Learn AngularJS in 1 Day

By Krishna Rungta

Table Of Content

Chapter 14: Events

1. The ng-click directive
2. Showing HTML Elements using ng-show
3. Hiding HTML Elements using ng-hide
4. AngularJS Event Listener Directives

Chapter 15: Routing with Parameters

1. Adding Angular Route ($routeProvider)
2. Creating a default route
3. Accessing parameters from the route
4. Using Angular $route service
5. Enabling HTML5 Routing

Chapter 16: AJAX Call

1. High-level interactions with servers using $resource
2. Low-level server interactions with $http
3. Fetching data from a server running SQL and MySQL

Chapter 17: Table

1. Populate & Display Data in a Table
2. AngularJS in-built Filter
3. Sort Table with OrderBy Filter
4. Display Table with Uppercase Filter
5. Display the Table Index ($index)

Chapter 18: Form Validation

1. Form validation using HTML5
2. Form validation using $dirty, $valid, $invalid, $pristine
3. Form validation using AngularJS Auto Validate
4. User feedbacks with Ladda buttons

Chapter 19: Form Submit

Chapter 20: ng-include

1. Client Side includes
2. Server Side Includes
3. How to include HTML file in AngularJS

Chapter 21: Dependency Injection

1. Which Component can be Injected as a Dependency In AngularJS
2. Example of Dependency Injection

Chapter 22: Karma Jasmine

1. Introduction & Installation of Karma framework
2. Testing AngularJS Controllers
3. Testing AngularJS Directives
4. End to End Testing AngularJS JS applications

Chapter 23: Protractor Testing

1. Why Do We Need Protractor Framework?
2. Protractor Installation
3. Sample AngularJS application testing using Protractor
4. Execution of the Code
5. Generate Reports using Jasmine Reporters

Chapter 1: What is AngularJS?

What is AngularJS?

AngularJS is an open source Model-View-Controller framework which is similar to the JavaScript framework.

Angular JS is probably one of the most popular modern day web frameworks available today. This framework is used for developing mostly Single Page applications. This framework has been developed by a group of developers from Google itself.

Because of the sheer support of Google and ideas from a wide community forum, the framework is always kept up to date. Also, it always incorporates the latest development trends in the market.

AngularJS Features

Angular has the following key features which makes it one of the powerful frameworks in the market.

1. **MVC** – The framework is built on the famous concept of MVC (Model-View-Controller). This is a design pattern used in all modern day web applications. This pattern is based on splitting the business logic layer, the data layer, and presentation layer into separate sections. The division into different sections is done so that each one could be managed more easily.

2. **Data Model Binding** – You don't need to write special code to bind data to the HTML controls. This can be done by Angular by just adding a few snippets of code.

3. **Writing less code** – When carrying out DOM manipulation a lot of JavaScript was required to be written to design any application. But with Angular, you will be amazed with the lesser amount of

code you need to write for DOM manipulation.

4. **Unit** Testing ready – The designers at Google not only developed Angular but also developed a testing framework called "Karma" which helps in designing unit tests for AngularJS applications.

AngularJS Architecture

Angular.js follows the MVC architecture, the diagram of the MVC framework as shown below.

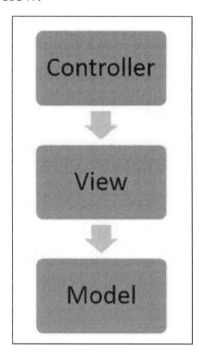

- The Controller represents the layer that has the business logic. User events trigger the functions which are stored inside your controller. The user events are part of the controller.

- Views are used to represent the presentation layer which is provided to the end users

- Models are used to represent your data. The data in your model can be as simple as just having primitive declarations. For example, if you are maintaining a student application, your data model could just have a student id and a name. Or it can also be complex by having a structured data model. If you are maintaining a car ownership application, you can have structures to define the vehicle itself in terms of its engine capacity, seating capacity, etc.

AngularJS Advantages

- Since it's an open source framework, you can expect the number of errors or issues to be minimal.

- Two-way binding – Angular.js keeps the data and presentation layer in sync. Now you don't need to write additional JavaScript code to keep the data in your HTML code and your data later in sync. Angular.js will automatically do this for you. You just need to specify which control is bound to which part of your model.

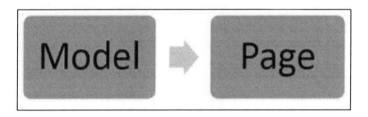

- Routing – Angular can take care of routing which means moving from one view to another. This is the key fundamental of single page applications; wherein you can move to different functionalities in your web application based on user interaction but still stay on the same page.

- Angular supports testing, both Unit Testing, and Integration Testing.

- It extends HTML by providing its own elements called directives. At a high level, directives are markers on a DOM element (such as an attribute, element name, and comment or CSS class) that tell AngularJS's HTML compiler to attach a specified behavior to that DOM element. These directives help in extending the functionality of existing HTML elements to give more power to your web application.

Chapter 2: Hello World

The best way to see the power of an AngularJS Application is to create your first basic program "Hello World" app in Angular.JS.

There are many integrated development environments you can use for AngularJS development, some of the popular ones are mentioned below. In our example, we are using Webstorm as our IDE.

1. Webstorm
2. Sublime Text
3. AngularJS Eclipse
4. Visual Studio

Hello world, AngularJS

The example below shows the easiest way to create your first "Hello world" application in AngularJS.

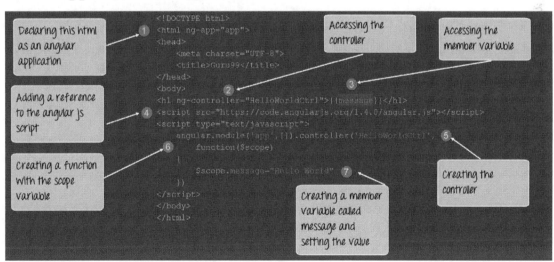

```
<!DOCTYPE html>
<html lang="en">
<head>
    <meta chrset="UTF 8">
    <title>Guru99</title>
</head>
```

```
<body ng-app="app">
<h1 ng-controller="HelloWorldCtrl">{{message}}</h1>
<script src="https://code.angularjs.org/1.6.9/angular.js">
</script>
<script>
    angular.module("app", []).controller("HelloWorldCtrl",
function($scope) {
    $scope.message="Hello World"
    } )
</script>

</body>
</html>
```

Code Explanation:

1. The "**ng-app**" keyword is used to denote that this application should be considered as an angular js application. Any name can be given to this application.

2. The controller is what is used to hold the business logic. In the h1 tag, we want to access the controller, which will have the logic to display "HelloWorld", so we can say, in this tag we want to access the controller named "HelloWorldCtrl".

3. We are using a member variable called "message" which is nothing but a placeholder to display the "Hello World" message.

4. The "script tag" is used to reference the angular.js script which has all the necessary functionality for angular js. Without this reference, if we try to use any AngularJS functions, they will not work.

5. "Controller" is the place where we are actually creating our business logic, which is our controller. The specifics of each keyword will be explained in the subsequent chapters. What is important to note that we are defining a controller method called 'HelloWorldCtrl' which is being referenced in Step2.

6. We are creating a "function" which will be called when our code calls this controller. The $scope object is a special object in AngularJS which is a global object used within Angular.js. The $scope object is used to manage the data between the controller and the view.

7. We are creating a member variable called "message", assigning it the value of "HelloWorld" and attaching the member variable to the scope object.

NOTE: The ng-controller directive is a keyword defined in AngularJS (step#2) and is used to define controllers in your application. Here in our application, we have used the ng-controller keyword to define a controller named 'HelloWorldCtrl'. The actual logic for the controller will be created in (step#5).

If the command is executed successfully, the following Output will be shown when you run your code in the browser.

Output:

The message 'Hello World' will be displayed.

Chapter 3: Controller

What is Controller in AngularJs?

A Controllers in AngularJs takes the data from the View, processes the data, and then sends that data across to the view which is displayed to the end user. The Controller will have your core business logic.

The controller will use the data model, carry out the required processing and then pass the output to the view which in turn is displayed to the end user.

What Controller does from Angular's perspective

Following is a simple definition of working of Angular JS Controller.

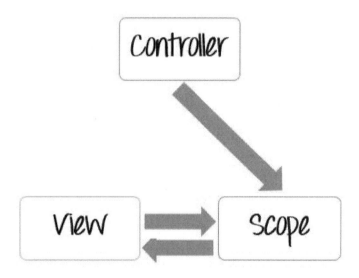

- The controller's primary responsibility is to control the data which gets passed to the view. The scope and the view have two-way communication.
- The properties of the view can call "functions" on the scope. Moreover events on the view can call "methods" on the scope. The

below code snippet gives a simple example of a function.

- ○ The function($scope) which is defined when defining the controller and an internal function which is used to return the concatenation of the $scope.firstName and $scope.lastName.
- ○ In AngularJS when you define a function as a variable, it is known as a Method.

```
app.controller('Ctrl', function($scope) {        Angular JS function

    $scope.firstName = "Guru";
    $scope.lastName = "99";
    $scope.fullName = function() {              methods - variables as function.

        return $scope.firstName + " " + $scope.lastName; }
```

- Data in this way pass from the controller to the scope, and then the data passes back and forth from the scope to the view.
- The scope is used to expose the model to the view. The model can be modified via methods defined in the scope which could be triggered via events from the view. We can define two way model binding from the scope to the model.
- Controllers should not ideally be used for manipulating the DOM. This should be done by the directives which we will see later on.
- Best practice is to have controller's based on functionality. For example, if you have a form for input and you need a controller for that, create a controller called "form controller".

How to build a basic Controller

Before we start with the creation of a controller, we need to first have our basic HTML page setup in place.

The below code snippet is a simple HTML page which has a title of "Event Registration" and has references to important libraries such as Bootstrap, jquery and Angular.

1. We are adding references to the bootstrap CSS stylesheets, which will be used in conjunction with the bootstrap libraries.
2. We are adding references to the angularjs libraries. So now whatever we do with angular.js going forward will be referenced from this library.
3. We are adding references to the bootstrap library to make our web page more responsive for certain controls.
4. We have added references to jquery libraries which will be used for DOM manipulation. This is required by Angular because some of the functionality in Angular is dependent on this library.

By default the above code snippet will be present in all of our examples, so that we can show just the specific angularJS code in the subsequent sections.

Secondly let's look at our files and file structure which we are going to start with for the duration of our course.

1. First we segregate our files into 2 folders as is done with any conventional web application. We have the "CSS" folder. It will contain all our cascading style sheet files, and then we will have

our "lib" folder which will have all our JavaScript files.

2. The bootstrap.css file is placed in the CSS folder and it used for adding a good look and feel for our website.

3. The angular.js is our main file which was downloaded from the angularJS site and kept in our lib folder.

4. The app.js file will contain our code for the controllers.

5. The bootstrap.js file is used to supplement the bootstrap.cs file to add bootstrap functionality to our web application.

6. The jquery file will be used to add DOM manipulation functionality to our site.

Let see an example on how to use angular.js,

What we want to do here is just to display the words "AngularJS" in both text format and in a text box when the page is viewed in the browser.

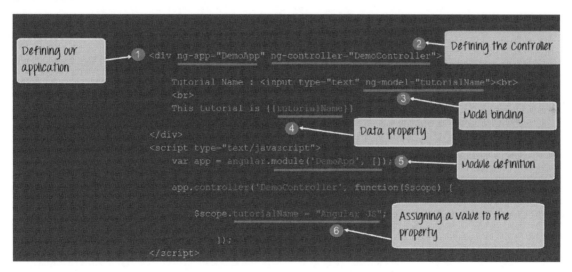

```html
<!DOCTYPE html>
<html>
<head>
        <meta chrset="UTF 8">
        <link rel="stylesheet" href="css/bootstrap.css"/>
</head>
<body>
<h1> Guru99 Global Event</h1>
<script src="https://code.angularjs.org/1.6.9/angular.js">
</script>
<script src="lib/angular.js"></script>
<script src="lib/bootstrap.js"></script>
```

```
<script src="lib/jquery-1.11.3.min.js"></script>

<div ng-app="DemoApp" ng-controller="DemoController">

        Tutorial Name : <input type="text" ng-
model="tutorialName"><br>

        This tutorial is {{tutorialName}}
</div>
<script>
        var app = angular.module('DemoApp',[]);

        app.controller('DemoController', function($scope){
        $scope.tutorialName = "Angular JS";
        });
</script>

</body>
</html>
```

Code Explanation:

1. The **ng-app** keyword is used to denote that this application should be considered as an angular application. Anything that starts with the prefix **'ng'** is known as a directive. "DemoApp" is the name given to our Angular.JS application.
2. We have created a div tag and in this tag we have added an ng-controller directive along with the name of our Controller "DemoController". This basically makes our div tag the ability to access the contents of the Demo Controller. You need to mention the name of the controller under the directive to ensure that you are able to access the functionality defined within the controller.
3. We are creating a model binding using the ng-model directive. What this does is that it binds the text box for Tutorial Name to be bound to the member variable "tutorialName".
4. We are creating a member variable called "tutorialName" which will be used to display the information which the user types in the text box for Tutorial Name.
5. We are creating a module which will attach to our DemoApp application. So this module now becomes part of our application.

6. In the module, we define a function which assigns a default value of "AngularJS" to our tutorialName variable.

If the command is executed successfully, the following Output will be shown when you run your code in the browser.

Output:

Since we assigned the variable tutorialName a value of "Angular JS", this gets displayed in the text box and in the plain text line.

How to define Methods in Controller

Normally, one would want to define multiple methods in the controller to separate the business logic.

For example, suppose if you wanted to have your controller do 2 basic things,

1. Perform the addition of 2 numbers
2. Perform the subtraction of 2 numbers

You would then ideally create 2 methods inside of your controller, one to perform the addition and the other to perform the subtraction.

One can define custom methods within an Angular.JS controller.

The example below shows how this can be done.

```
<div ng-app="DemoApp" ng-controller="DemoController">

    Tutorial Name : <input type="text" ng-model="tutorialName"><br>
    <br>
    This tutorial is {{tutorialName}}

</div>
<script type="text/javascript">
    var app = angular.module('DemoApp', []);
        app.controller('DemoController', function($scope) {
        $scope.tutorialName = function(){
            return "Angular JS";
        };

    });
</script>
```

using a module to populate the member variable with a value

```html
<!DOCTYPE html>
<html>
<head>
        <meta chrset="UTF 8">
        <title>Event Registration</title>
        <link rel="stylesheet" href="css/bootstrap.css"/>
</head>
<body ng-app="DemoApp">
<h1> Guru99 Global Event</h1>
<script src="https://code.angularjs.org/1.6.9/angular.js">
</script>
<script src="lib/angular.js"></script>
<script src="lib/bootstrap.js"></script>
<script src="lib/jquery-1.11.3.min.js"></script>

<div ng-app="DemoApp" ng-controller="DemoController">
        Tutorial Name :<input type="text" ng-
model="tutorialName"><br>
        <br>
        This tutorial is {{tutorialName}}
</div>

<script>
var app = angular.module('DemoApp', []);
app.controller('DemoController', function($scope) {
    $scope.tutorialName = "Angular JS";
        $scope.tName = function() {
        return $scope.tName;
    };
});
```

```
</script>
</body>
</html>
```

Code Explanation:

1. Here, we are just defining a function which returns a string of "AngularJS". The function is attached to the scope object via a member variable called tutorialName.
2. If the command is executed successfully, the following Output will be shown when you run your code in the browser.

Output:

Using ng-controller in External Files

Let's look at an example of "HelloWorld" where all of the functionality was placed in a single file. Now it's time to place the code for the controller in separate files.

Let's follow the steps below to do this.

Step 1) In the app.js file, add the following code for your controller

```
angular.module('app',
[]).controller('HelloWorldCtrl',function($scope)
{
        $scope.message = "Hello World"
});
```

The above code does the following things,

1. Define a module called "app" which will hold the controller along with the controller functionality.
2. Create a controller with the name "HelloWorldCtrl". This controller will be used to have a functionality to display a "Hello World" message.
3. The scope object is used to pass information from the controller to the view. So in our case, the scope object will be used to hold a variable called "message".
4. We are defining the variable message and assigning the value "Hello World" to it.

Step 2) Now, in your Sample.html file add a div class which will contain the ng-controller directive and then add a reference to the member variable "message"

Also don't forget to add a reference to the script file app.js which has the source code for your controller.

Add a div tag which will have the controller tag and add the message member

Add a reference to the app.js file

```html
<!DOCTYPE html>
<html ng-app="app">
<head>
        <meta chrset="UTF 8">
        <title>Event Registration</title>
        <link rel="stylesheet" href="css/bootstrap.css"/>
</head>
<body>
<h1> Guru99 Global Event</h1>
<div class="container">
        <div ng-controller="HelloWorldCtrl">{{message}}</div>
</div>

<script src="https://code.angularjs.org/1.6.9/angular.js">
</script>
<script src="lib/angular.js"></script>
<script src="lib/bootstrap.js"></script>
<script src="lib/jquery-1.11.3.min.js"></script>

<script src="app.js"></script>

</body>
</html>
```

If the above code is entered correctly, the following Output will be shown when you run your code in the browser.

Output:

Summary

- The controller's primary responsibility is to create a scope object which in turn gets passed to the view
- How to build a simple controller using the ng-app, ng-controller and ng-model directives
- How to add custom methods to a controller which can be used to separate various functionalities within an angularjs module.
- Controllers can be defined in external files to separate this layer from the View layer. This is normally a best practice when creating web applications.

Chapter 4: What is $Scope in AngularJS?

What is $scope in AngularJS?

The scope is a JavaScript object which basically binds the "controller" and the "view". One can define member variables in the scope within the controller which can then be accessed by the view.

Consider example below:

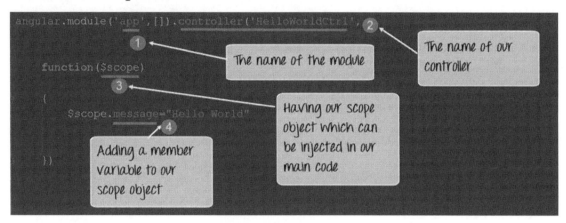

```
angular.module('app',[]).controller(
        function($scope)
        {
                $scope.message = "Hello World"
        });
```

Code Explanation:

From the above code snippet you can see that we can define multiple member variables like tutorial name, name, topic, etc. and assign them the relevant values.

In our div tag, we can the display these values accordingly. Hence as we mentioned before the scope object is the main object which is used to pass information from the controller to the view.

Setting up or adding Behavior

In order to react to events or execute some sort of computation/processing in the View, we must provide behavior to the scope.

Behaviors are added to scope objects to respond to specific events that may be triggered by the View. Once the behavior is defined in the controller, it can be accessed by the view.

Let's look at an example of how we can achieve this.

```html
<!DOCTYPE html>
<html lang="en">
<head>
    <meta chrset="UTF 8">
    <title>Guru99</title>
</head>
<body ng-app="DemoApp">
<h1> Guru99 Global Event</h1>
<script src="https://code.angularjs.org/1.6.9/angular.js">
</script>
<div ng-controller="DemoController">
        {{fullName("Guru","99")}}
</div>
<script type="text/javascript">
        var app = angular.module("DemoApp", []);
        app.controller("DemoController", function($scope) {

    $scope.fullName=function(firstName,lastname){
            return firstName + lastname;
```

```
                    }
          } );
</script>

</body>
</html>
```

Code Explanation:

1. We are creating a behavior called "fullName". This behavior is a function which accepts 2 parameters (firstName,lastname).
2. The behavior then returns the concatenation of these 2 parameters.
3. In the view we are calling the behavior and passing in 2 values of "Guru" and "99" which gets passed as parameters to the behavior.

If the command is executed successfully, the following Output will be shown when you run your code in the browser.

Output:

In the browser you will see a concatenation of both the values of Guru & 99 which were passed to the behavior in the controller.

Summary

- Various member variables can be added to the scope object which can then be referenced in the view.
- Behavior can be added to work with events which are generated for actions performed by the user.

Chapter 5: ng-repeat Directive

Displaying repeated information

Sometimes we may be required to display a list of items in the view, so the question is that how can we display a list of items defined in our controller onto our view page.

Angular provides a directive called "ng-repeat" which can be used to display repeating values defined in our controller.

Let's look at an example of how we can achieve this.

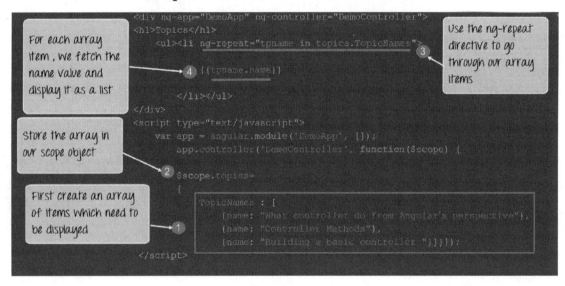

```
<!DOCTYPE html>
<html>
<head>
        <meta chrset="UTF 8">
        <title>Event Registration</title>
        <link rel="stylesheet" href="css/bootstrap.css"/>
</head>
<body >
<h1> Guru99 Global Event</h1>
<script src="https://code.angularjs.org/1.6.9/angular.js">
</script>

<div ng-app="DemoApp" ng-controller="DemoController">
<h1>Topics</h1>
<ul><li ng-repeat="tpname in TopicNames">
```

```
                    {{tpname.name}}
                    </li></ul>
</div>

<script>
        var app = angular.module('DemoApp',[]);
        app.controller('DemoController', function($scope){

        $scope.TopicNames =[
                {name: "What controller do from Angular's
perspective"},
                {name: "Controller Methods"},
                {name: "Building a basic controller"}];
                });
</script>

</body>
</html>
```

Code Explanation:

1. In the controller, we first define our array of list items which we want to define in the view. Over here we have defined an array called "TopicNames" which contains three items. Each item consists of a name-value pair.

2. The array of TopicsNames is then added to a member variable called "topics" and attached to our scope object.

3. We are using the HTML tags of <ul>(Unordered List) and <li> (List Item) to display the list of items in our array. We then use the ng-repeat directive for going through each and every item in our array. The word "tpname" is a variable which is used to point to each item in the array topics.TopicNames.

4. In this, we will display the value of each array item.

If the code is executed successfully, the following Output will be shown when you run your code in the browser. You will see all items of the array (Basically the TopicNames in topics) displayed.

Output:

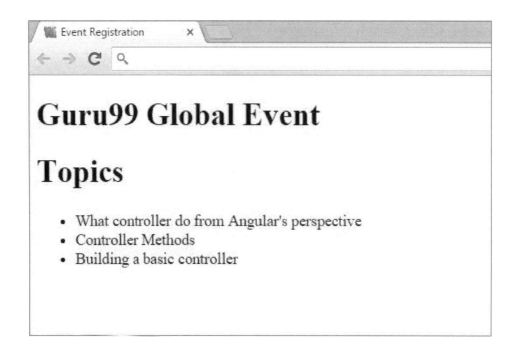

Angularjs Multiple Controllers

An advanced controller example would be the concept of having multiple controllers in an angular JS application.

You might want to define multiple controllers to separate different business logic functions. Earlier we mentioned about having different methods in a controller in which one method had separate functionality for addition and subtraction of numbers. Well, you can have multiple controllers to have a more advanced separation of logic. For example, you can have one controller which does just operations on numbers and the other which does operations on strings.

Let's look at an example of how we can define multiple controllers in an angular.JS application.

```html
<!DOCTYPE html>
<html>
<head>
        <meta chrset="UTF 8">
        <title>Event Registration</title>
        <link rel="stylesheet" href="css/bootstrap.css"/>
</head>
<body >
<h1> Guru99 Global Event</h1>
<script src="https://code.angularjs.org/1.6.9/angular.js">
</script>

<div ng-app="DemoApp">
        <div ng-controller="firstcontroller">
                <div ng-controller="secondcontroller">
                {{lname}}
                </div>
        </div>
</div>

<script>
        var app = angular.module('DemoApp',[]);
        app.controller('firstcontroller', function($scope){
                $scope.pname="firstcontroller";
                        });
                app.controller('secondcontroller',
function($scope){
                        $scope.lname="secondcontroller";
                        });
</script>
</body>
</html>
```

Code Explanation:

1. Here we are defining 2 controllers called "firstController" and "secondController". For each controller we are also adding some code for processing. In our firstController , we attach a variable called "pname" which has the value "firstController", and in the secondController we attach a variable called "lname" which has the value "secondController".
2. In the view, we are accessing both controllers and using the member variable from the second controller.

If the code is executed successfully, the following Output will be shown when you run your code in the browser. You will see all text of "secondController" as expected.

Output:

Summary

- The ng-repeater directive can be used to display multiple repeating items.
- We also had a look at an advanced controller which looked at the definition of multiple controllers in an application.

Chapter 6: How to use "ng-model"

What is ng-model in AngularJs?

ng-model is a directive in Angular.JS that represents models and its primary purpose is to bind the "view" to the "model".

For example, suppose you wanted to present a simple page to the end user like the one shown below which asks the user to enter the "First name" and "Last name" in textboxes. And then you wanted to ensure that you store the information that the user has entered in your data model.

You can use the ng-model directive to map the text box fields of "First name" and "Last Name" to your data model.

The ng-model directive will ensure that the data in the "view" and that of your "model" are kept in sync the whole time.

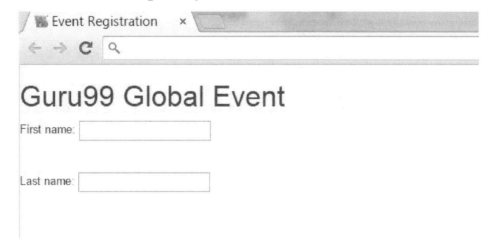

The ng-model Attribute

As discussed in the introduction to this chapter, the ng-model attribute is used to bind the data in your model to the view presented to the user.

The ng-model attribute is used for,

1. Binding controls such as input, text area and selects in the view into the model.
2. Provide a validation behavior - for example, a validation can be added to a text box that only numeric characters can be entered into the text box.
3. The ng-model attribute maintains the state of the control (By state, we mean that the control and the data is bound to be always kept in sync. If the value of our data changes, it will automatically change the value in the control and vice versa)

How to use ng-model

1) Text Area

The text area tag is used to define a multi-line text input control. The text area can hold an unlimited number of characters, and the text renders in a fixed-width font.

So now let's look at a simple example of how we can add the ng-model directive to a text area control.

In this example, we want to show how we can pass a multiline string from the controller to the view and attach that value to the text area control.

```
<!DOCTYPE html>
<html>
<head>
        <meta chrset="UTF 8">
        <title>Event Registration</title>
        <link rel="stylesheet" href="css/bootstrap.css"/>
</head>
<body >
<h1> Guru99 Global Event</h1>
<script src="https://code.angularjs.org/1.6.9/angular.js">
</script>

<div ng-app="DemoApp" ng-controller="DemoCtrl">
        <form>
                   Topic Description:<br> <br>
                   
        <textarea rows="4" cols="50" ng-model="pDescription">
</textarea><br><br>
        </form>
</div>

<script>
        var app = angular.module('DemoApp',[]);
        app.controller('DemoCtrl', function($scope){
                $scope.pDescription="This topic looks at how
Angular JS works \nModels in Angular JS"});
</script>

</body>
</html>
```

Code Explanation:

1. The **ng-model directive** is used to attach the member variable called "pDescription" to the "textarea" control.

    The "pDescription" variable will actually contain the text, which will be passed on to the text area control. We have also mentioned 2 attributes for the textarea control which is rows=4 and cols=50. These attributes have been mentioned so that we can show multiple lines of text. By defining these attributes the textarea will now have 4 rows and 50 columns so that it can show multiple lines of text.

2. Here we are attaching the member variable to the scope object called "pDescription" and putting a string value to the variable.

3. Note that we are putting the /n literal in the string so that the text can be of multiple lines when it is displayed in the text area. The /n literal splits the text into multiple lines so that it can render in the textarea control as multiple lines of text.

If the code is executed successfully, the following Output will be shown when you run the code in the browser.

Output:

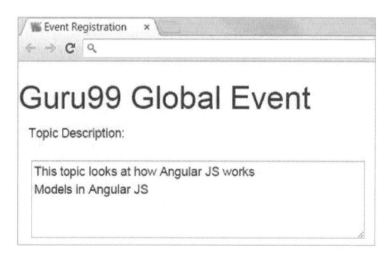

From the output

-   It can be clearly seen that the value assigned to the pDescription variable as part of the scope object was passed to the textarea control.

- Subsequently, it has been displayed when the page is loaded.

2) Input elements

The ng-model directive can also be applied to the input elements such as the text box, checkboxes, radio buttons, etc.

Let's look at an example of how we can use the ng-model with the "textbox" and "checkbox" input type.

Here we will have a text input type which will have the name of "Guru99" and there will be 2 checkboxes, one which will be marked by default and the other will not be marked.

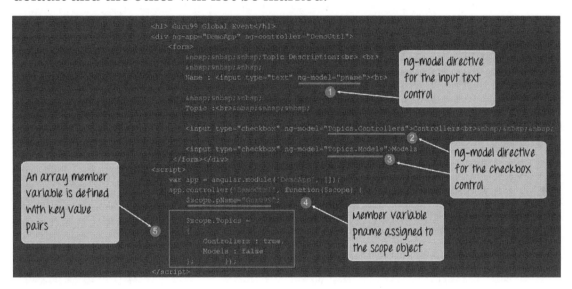

```
<!DOCTYPE html>
<html>
<head>
        <meta chrset="UTF 8">
        <title>Event Registration</title>
        <link rel="stylesheet" href="css/bootstrap.css"/>
        <script
src="https://code.angularjs.org/1.6.9/angular.js"></script>
</head>
<body >
<h1> Guru99 Global Event</h1>

<div ng-app="DemoApp" ng-controller="DemoCtrl">
        <form>
                   Topic Description:<br> <br>
                   
```

```
                Name : <input type="text" ng-model="pname"><br>
                   
                Topic : <br>   
                <input type="checkbox" ng-
model="Topic.Controller">Controller<br>   
                <input type="checkbox" ng-
model="Topic.Models">Models
        </form>
        </div>

<script>
        var app = angular.module('DemoApp',[]);
        app.controller('DemoCtrl', function($scope){
                $scope.pname="Guru99";

                $scope.Topic =
                {
                        Controller:true,
                        Models:false
                };      });
</script>

</body>
</html>
```

Code Explanation:

1. The **ng-model directive** is used to attach the member variable called "pname" to the input type text control. The "pname" variable will contain the text of "Guru99" which will be passed on to the text input control. Note that any name can be given to the name of the member variable.

2. Here we are defining our first checkbox "Controllers" which is attached to the member variable Topics.Controllers. The checkbox will be marked for this check control.

3. Here we are defining our first checkbox "Models" which is attached to the member variable Topics.Models. The checkbox will not be marked for this check control.

4. Here we are attaching the member variable called "pName" and putting a string value of "Guru99".

5. We are declaring a member array variable called "Topics" and

giving it two values, the first is "true" and the second is "false".

So when the first checkbox gets the value of true, the check-box will be marked for this control, and likewise, since the second value is false, the check-box will not be marked for this control.

If the code is executed successfully, the following Output will be shown when you run your code in the browser.

Output:

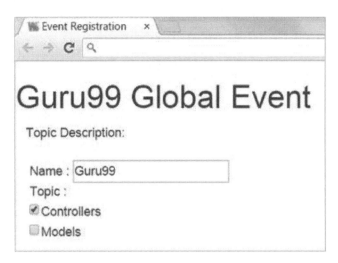

From the output,

- It can be clearly seen that the value assigned to the pName variable is "Guru99"
- Since the first check value is "true" it passed, the checkbox is marked for the "Controllers" checkbox. Likewise since the second value is false, the checkbox is not marked for the "Models" checkbox.

3) Select element form Dropdown

The ng-model directive can also be applied to the select element and be used to populate the list items in the select list.

Let's look at an example of how we can use the ng-model with the select input type.

Here we will have a text input type which will have the name of "Guru99" and there will be a select list with 2 list items of "Controller" and "Models".

```
<h1> Guru99 Global Event</h1>
<div ng-app="DemoApp" ng-controller="DemoCtrl">
    <form>
           Topic Description:<br> <br>
           
        Name : <input type="text" ng-model="pname" value="Guru99"><br>
           
        Topic :<br>   

        <select ng-model="Topics">
        <option>{{Topics.option1}}</option>
        <option>{{Topics.option2}}</option>
        </select>
    </form></div>
<script>
    var app = angular.module('DemoApp', []);
    app.controller('DemoCtrl', function($scope) {
        $scope.pName="Guru99";

        $scope.Topics =
        {
            option1 : "Controllers",
            option2 : "Models"
        };        });
</script>
```

1 — select input control with the ng-model directive

2 — Array member variable to hold the select options

```
<!DOCTYPE html>
<html>
<head>
        <meta chrset="UTF 8">
        <title>Event Registration</title>
        <link rel="stylesheet" href="css/bootstrap.css"/>
        <script
src="https://code.angularjs.org/1.6.9/angular.js"></script>
</head>
<body >
<h1> Guru99 Global Event</h1>

<div ng-app="DemoApp" ng-controller="DemoCtrl">
        <form>
                   Topic Description:<br> <br>
                   

                Name : <input type="text" ng-model="pName"
value="Guru99"><br>
                   
                Topic : <br>   
```

```
              <select ng-model="Topics">
              <option>{{Topics.option1}}</option>
              <option>{{Topics.option2}}</option>
              </select>
        </form>
        </div>

<script>
        var app = angular.module('DemoApp',[]);
        app.controller('DemoCtrl', function($scope){
        $scope.pName="Guru99";

              $scope.Topics =
              {
                     option1 : "Controller",
                     option2 : "Module"
              };       });
</script>

</body>
</html>
```

1. The **ng-model directive** is used to attach the member variable called "Topics" to the select type control. Inside of the select control, for each of the options, we are attaching the member variable of Topics.option1 for the first option and Topics.option2 for the second option.

2. Here we are defining our Topics array variable which holds 2 key-value pairs. The first pair has a value of "Controllers" and the second has the value of "Models". These values will be passed to select input tag in the view.

   If the code is executed successfully, the following Output will be shown.

Output:

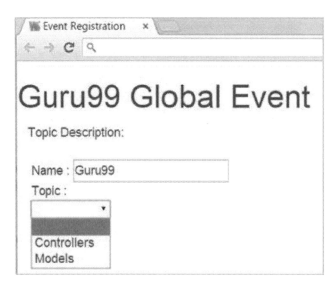

From the output, it can be seen that the value assigned to the pName variable is "Guru99" and we can see that the select input control has the options of "Controllers" and "Models".

Summary

- Models in Angular JS are represented by the ng-model directive. The primary purpose of this directive is to bind the view to the model. How to build a simple controller using the ng-app, ng-controller and ng-model directives.
- The ng-model directive can be linked to a "text area" input control and multiline strings can be passed from the controller to the view.
- The ng-model directive can be linked to input controls like the text and checkbox controls to make them more dynamic at run time.
- The ng-model directive can also be used to populate a select list with options which can be displayed to the user.

Chapter 7: ng-view

Nowadays, everyone would have heard about the "Single Page Applications". Many of the well-known websites such as Gmail use the concept of Single Page Applications (SPA's).

SPA's is the concept wherein when a user requests for a different page, the application will not navigate to that page but instead display the view of the new page within the existing page itself.

It gives the feeling to the user that he never left the page in the first place. The same can be achieved in the Angular with the help of Views in conjunction with Routes.

What is a View?

A view is the content which is shown to the user. Basically what the user wants to see, accordingly that view of the application will be shown to the user.

The combination of views and Routes helps one into dividing an application in logical views and bind different views to Controllers.

Dividing the application into different views and using Routing to load different part of application helps in logically dividing the application and making it more manageable.

Let's assume that we have an ordering application, wherein a customer can view orders and place new ones.

The below diagram and subsequent explanation demonstrate how to make this application as a single page application.

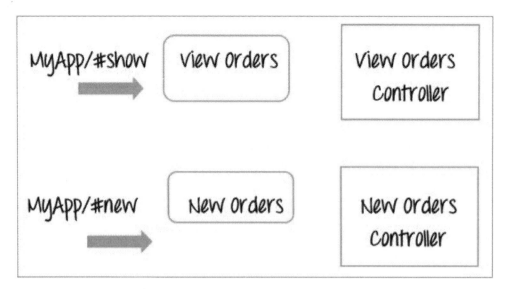

Now, instead of having two different web pages, one for "View orders" and another for "New Orders", in AngularJS, you would instead create two different views called "View Orders" and "New Orders" in the same page.

We will also have 2 reference links in our application called #show and #new.

- So when the application goes to MyApp/#show, it will show the view of the View Orders, at the same time it will not leave the page. It will just refresh the section of the existing page with the information of "View Orders". The same goes for the "New Orders" view.

So in this way it just becomes simpler to separate the application into different views to make it more manageable and easy to make changes whenever required.

And each view will have a corresponding controller to control the business logic for that functionality.

ng-view Directive in AngularJS

The "ngView" is a directive that complements the $route service by including the rendered template of the current route into the main layout (index.html) file.

Every time the current route changes, the view included changes to it according to the configuration of the $route service without changing the page itself.

We will be covering routes in a later chapter, for now, we will focus on adding multiple views to our application.

Below is the entire flowchart of how the entire process works. We will go through in detail for every process in our example shown below.

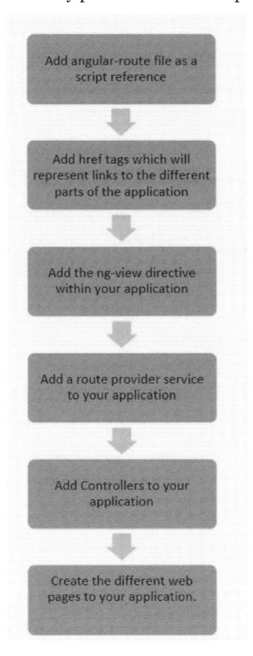

ng-view Example

Let's take a look at an example of how we can implement views.

In our example, we are going to present two options to the user,

- One is to Display an "Event", and the other is to add an "Event".
- When the user clicks on the Add an Event link, they will be shown the view for "Add Event" and the same goes for "Display Event."

Please follow the steps below to get this example in place.

Step 1) Include the angular-route file as a script reference.

This route file is necessary in order to make use of the functionalities of having multiple routes and views. This file can be downloaded from the angularJS website.

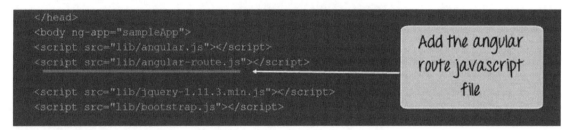

```
</head>
<body ng-app="sampleApp">
<script src="lib/angular.js"></script>
<script src="lib/angular-route.js"></script>

<script src="lib/jquery-1.11.3.min.js"></script>
<script src="lib/bootstrap.js"></script>
```

Add the angular route javascript file

Step 2) In this step,

1. Add href tags which will represent links to "Adding a New Event" and "Displaying an Event".
2. Also, add a div tag with the ng-view directive which will represent the view.

   This will allow the corresponding view to be injected whenever the user clicks on either the "Add New Event link" or the "Display Event link."

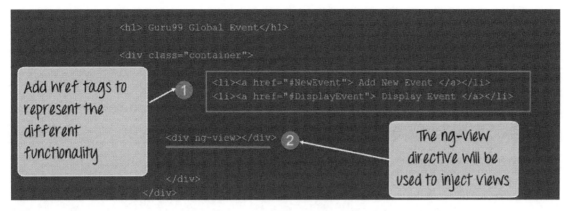

```
<h1> Guru99 Global Event</h1>

<div class="container">

    <li><a href="#NewEvent"> Add New Event </a></li>
    <li><a href="#DisplayEvent"> Display Event </a></li>

    <div ng-view></div>

</div>
</div>
```

Add href tags to represent the different functionality ①

② The ng-view directive will be used to inject views

Step 3) In your script tag for Angular JS, add the following code.

Let's not worry about the routing, for now, we will see this in a later chapter. Let's just see the code for the views for now.

1. This section of code means that when the user clicks on the href tag "NewEvent" which was defined in the div tag earlier. It will go to the web page add_event.html, and will take the code from there and inject it into the view. Secondly for processing the business logic for this view, go to the "AddEventController".

2. This section of code means that when the user clicks on the href tag "DisplayEvent" which was defined in the div tag earlier. It will go to the web page show_event.html, take the code from there and inject it into the view. Secondly, for processing the business logic for this view, go to the "ShowDisplayController".

3. This section of code means that the default view shown to the user is the DisplayEvent view

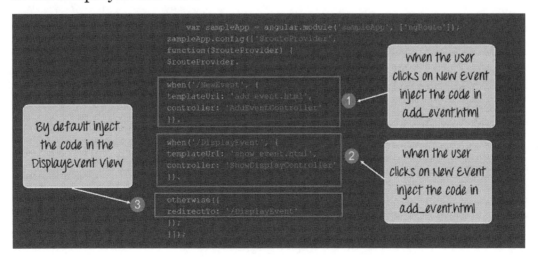

By default inject the code in the DisplayEvent View ③

① When the user clicks on New Event inject the code in add_event.html

② When the user clicks on New Event inject the code in add_event.html

Step 4) Next is to add controllers to process the business logic for both the "DisplayEvent" and "Add New Event" functionality.

We are just simply adding a message variable to each scope object for each controller. This message will get displayed when the appropriate view is shown to the user.

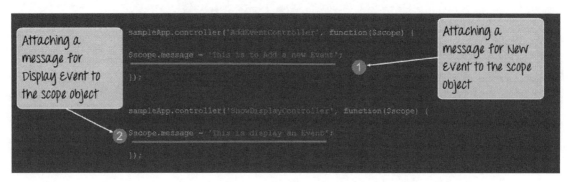

```
<!DOCTYPE html>
<html>
<head>
    <meta chrset="UTF 8">
    <title>Event Registration</title>
    <script src="https://code.angularjs.org/1.5.9/angular-
route.js"></script>
    <script
src="https://code.angularjs.org/1.5.9/angular.min.js"></script>
    <script src="lib/bootstrap.js"></script>

</head>
<body ng-app="sampleApp">

<h1> Guru99 Global Event</h1>

<div class="container">
    <ul><li><a href="#!NewEvent"> Add New Event</a></li>
        <li><a href="#!DisplayEvent"> Display Event</a></li>
    </ul>
    <div ng-view></div>
</div>

<script>
    var app = angular.module('sampleApp',["ngRoute"]);
    app.config(function($routeProvider){
        $routeProvider.
        when("/NewEvent",{
            templateUrl : "add_event.html",
            controller: "AddEventController"
```

```
    }).
    when("/DisplayEvent", {
        templateUrl: "show_event.html",
        controller: "ShowDisplayController"
    }).
    otherwise ({
        redirectTo: '/DisplayEvent'
    });
});
app.controller("AddEventController", function($scope) {

    $scope.message = "This is to Add a new Event";

});
app.controller("ShowDisplayController",function($scope){

    $scope.message = "This is display an Event";

});
</script>
</body>
</html>
```

Step 5) Create pages called add_event.html and show_event.html.
Keep the pages simple as shown below.

In our case, the add_event.html page will have a header tag along with
the text "Add New Event" and have an expression to display the
message "This is to Add a new Event".

Similarly, the show_event.html page will also have a header tag to hold
the text "Show Event" and also have a message expression to display
the message "This is to display an Event."

The value of the message variable will be injected based on the
controller which is attached to the view.

For each page, we are going to add the message variable, which will be
injected from each respective controller.

- **add_event.html**

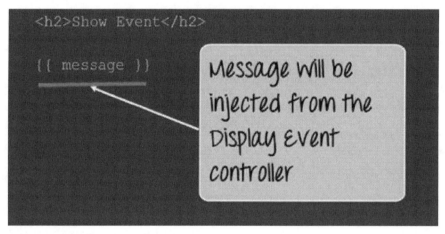

```
<h2>Add New Event</h2>

{{message}}
```

- **show_event.html**

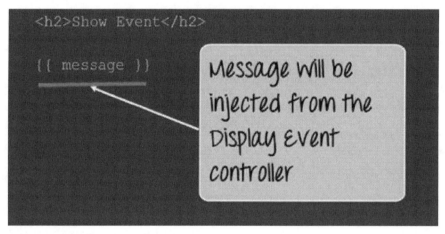

```
<h2>Show Event</h2>

{{message}}
```

If the code is executed successfully, the following Output will be shown when you run your code in the browser.

Output:

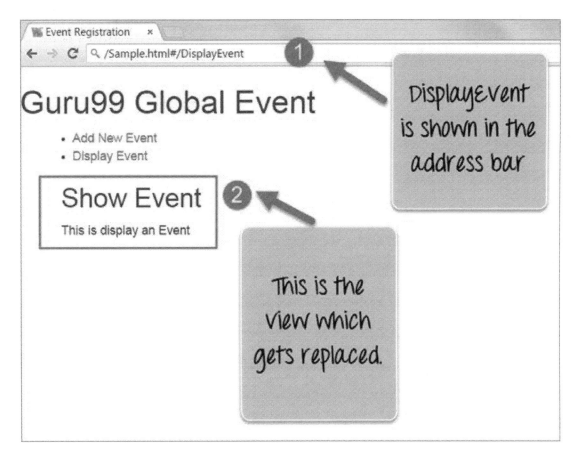

From the output, we can notice 2 things

1. The address bar will reflect what is the current view being displayed. So since the default view is to show the Show Event screen, the address bar shows the address for "DisplayEvent".

2. This section is the View, which gets created on the fly. Since the default view is the Show Event one, this is what gets displayed to the user.

Now click on the Add New Event link in the page displayed. You will now get the below output.

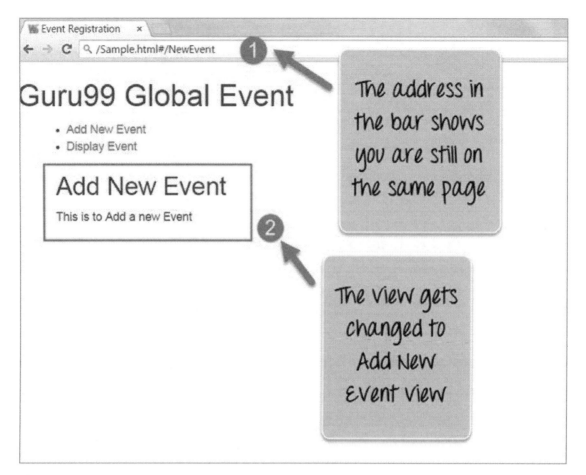

Output:

1. The address bar will now reflect that the current view is now the "Add new Event" view. Notice that you will still be on the same application page. You will not be directed to a new application page.

2. This section is the View, and it will now change to show the HTML for the "Add new event" functionality. So now in this section the header tag "Add New Event" and the text "This is to Add a new Event" is displayed to the user.

Chapter 8: Expressions

What is Angular JS Expressions?

Expressions are variables which were defined in the double braces {{ }}. They are very commonly used within Angular JS, and you would see them in our previous tutorials.

Explain Angular.js Expressions with an example

AngularJS expressions are those that are written inside double braces {{expression}}.

Syntax:

A simple example of an expression is {{5 + 6}}.

Angular.JS expressions are used to bind data to HTML the same way as the ng-bind directive. AngularJS displays the data exactly at the place where the expression is placed.

Let's look at an example of Angular.JS expressions.

In this example, we just want to show a simple addition of numbers as an expression.

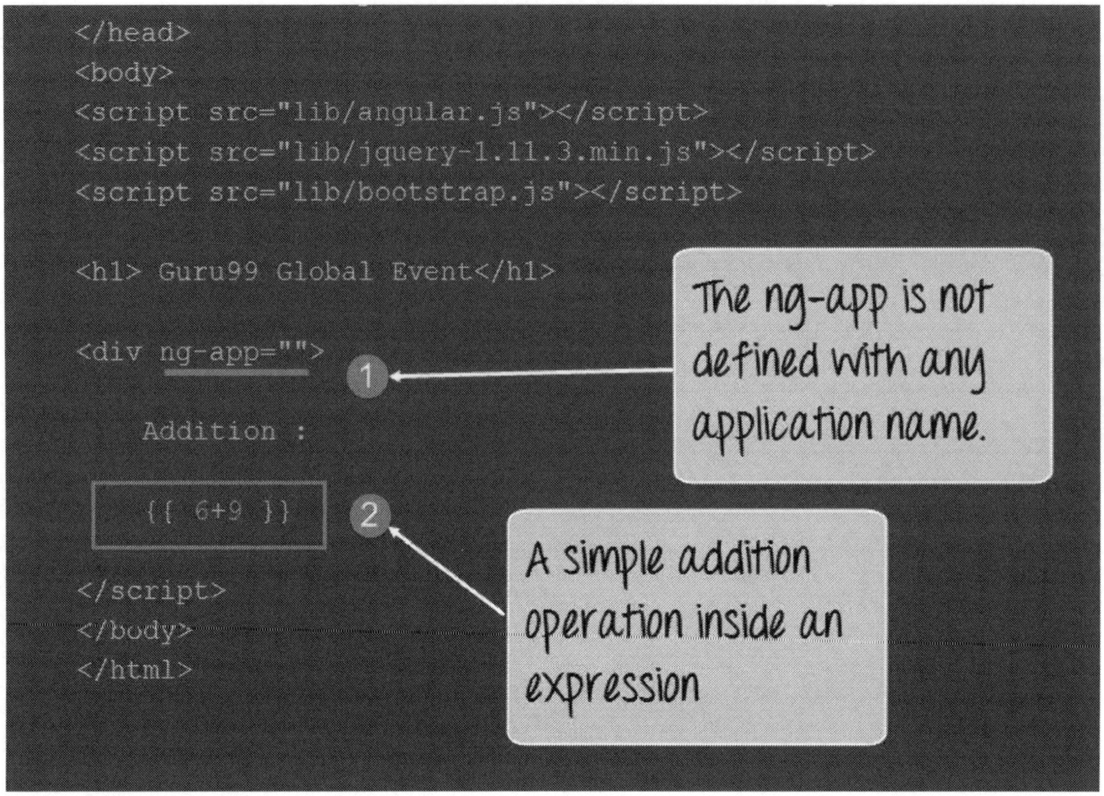

```
</head>
<body>
<script src="lib/angular.js"></script>
<script src="lib/jquery-1.11.3.min.js"></script>
<script src="lib/bootstrap.js"></script>

<h1> Guru99 Global Event</h1>

<div ng-app="">

    Addition :

    {{ 6+9 }}

</script>
</body>
</html>
```

1 → The ng-app is not defined with any application name.

2 → A simple addition operation inside an expression

```
<!DOCTYPE html>
<html>
<head>
    <meta chrset="UTF 8">
    <title>Event Registration</title>

</head>
<body>

    <script src="https://code.angularjs.org/1.6.9/angular-
route.js"></script>
    <script
src="https://code.angularjs.org/1.6.9/angular.min.js"></script>

    <h1> Guru99 Global Event</h1>

    <div ng-app="">
        Addition : {{6+9}}
    </div>

</body>
</html>
```

Code Explanation:

1. The ng-app directive in our example is blank as shown in above screenshot. This only means that there is no module to assign controllers, directives, services attached to the code.
2. We are adding a simple expression which looks at the addition of 2 numbers.

If the code is executed successfully, the following Output will be shown when you run your code in the browser.

Output:

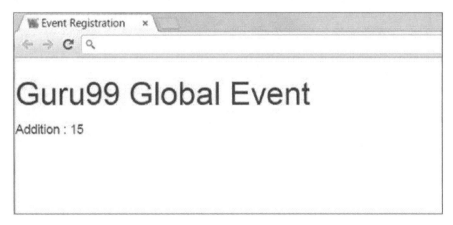

From the output,

- It can be seen that the addition of the two numbers 9 and 6 take place and the added value of 15 is displayed.

Angular.JS Numbers

Expressions can be used to work with numbers as well. Let's look at an example of Angular.JS expressions with numbers.

In this example, we just want to show a simple multiplication of 2 number variables called margin and profit and displayed their multiplied value.

```
</head>
<body>
<script src="lib/angular.js"></script>
<script src="lib/jquery-1.11.3.min.js"></script>
<script src="lib/bootstrap.js"></script>

<h1> Guru99 Global Event</h1>

<div ng-app="" ng-init="margin=2;profit=200">     1

    Total Profir margin

    {{ margin*profit }}        2

</script>
</body>
</html>
```

1 ng-init tag to initialize variables

2 variables being used in an expression

```
<!DOCTYPE html>
<html>
<head>
    <meta chrset="UTF 8">
    <title>Event Registration</title>

</head>
<body>

    <script src="https://code.angularjs.org/1.6.9/angular-
route.js"></script>
    <script
src="https://code.angularjs.org/1.6.9/angular.min.js"></script>

    <h1> Guru99 Global Event</h1>

    <div ng-app="" ng-init="margin=2;profit=200">
        Total profit margin

        {{margin*profit}}
    </div>

</body>
</html>
```

Code Explanation:

1. The ng-init directive is used in angular.js to define variables and

their corresponding values in the view itself. It's somewhat like defining local variables to code in any programming language. In this case, we are defining 2 variables called margin and profit and assigning values to them.

2. We are then using the 2 local variables and multiplying their values.

If the code is executed successfully, the following Output will be shown when you run your code in the browser.

Output:

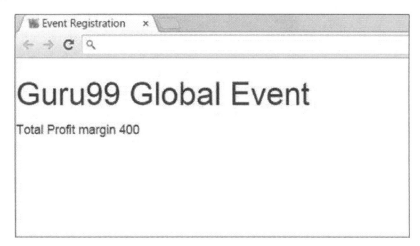

From the output,

*   It can be clearly seen that the multiplication of the 2 numbers 2 and 200 take place, and the multiplied value of 400 is displayed.

AngularJS Strings

Expressions can be used to work with strings as well. Let's look at an example of Angular JS expressions with strings.

In this example, we are going to define 2 strings of "firstName" and "lastName" and display them using expressions accordingly.

```
</head>
<body>
<script src="lib/angular.js"></script>
<script src="lib/jquery-1.11.3.min.js"></script>
<script src="lib/bootstrap.js"></script>

<h1> Guru99 Global Event</h1>

<div ng-app="" ng-init="firstName='Guru';lastName='99'">    ①

       
    First Name : {{ firstName }}<br>   
    Last Name  : {{ lastName }}                                 ②

</script>
</body>
</html>
```

ng-init tag to initialize string variables

Variables names being displayed.

```html
<!DOCTYPE html>
<html>
<head>
    <meta chrset="UTF 8">
    <title>Event Registration</title>

</head>
<body>

    <script src="https://code.angularjs.org/1.6.9/angular-
route.js"></script>
    <script
src="https://code.angularjs.org/1.6.9/angular.min.js"></script>

    <h1> Guru99 Global Event</h1>

    <div ng-app="" ng-init="firstName='Guru';lastName='99'">

           
        First Name : {{firstName}}<br>   
        last Name : {{lastName}}

    </div>

</body>
</html>
```

Code Explanation:

1. The ng-init directive is used define the variables firstName with the value "Guru" and the variable lastName with the value of "99".

2. We are then using expressions of {{firstName}} and {{lastName}} to access the value of these variables and display them in the view accordingly.

If the code is executed successfully, the following Output will be shown when you run your code in the browser.

Output:

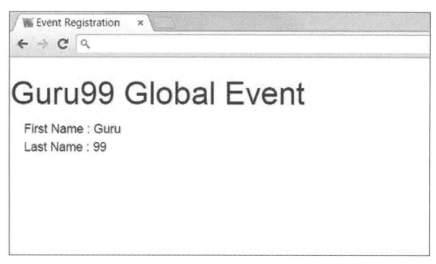

From the output, it can be clearly seen that the values of firstName and lastName are displayed on the screen.

Angular.JS Objects

Expressions can be used to work with JavaScript objects as well.

Let's look at an example of Angular.JS expressions with javascript objects. A javascript object consists of a name-value pair.

Below is an example of the syntax of a javascript object.

Syntax:

```
var car = {type:"Ford", model:"Explorer", color:"White"};
```

In this example, we are going to define one object as a person object which will have 2 key value pairs of "firstName" and "lastName".

```
</head>
<body>
<script src="lib/angular.js"></script>
<script src="lib/jquery-1.11.3.min.js"></script>
<script src="lib/bootstrap.js"></script>

<h1> Guru99 Global Event</h1>

<div ng-app="" ng-init="person={firstName:'Guru',lastName:'99'}">
```
①   Creating an object variable with 2 key value pairs

```
       
    First Name : {{ person.firstName }}<br>   

    Last Name  : {{ person.lastName }}
```
②   Accessing each value of the object person via it's key value pairs

```
</script>
</body>
</html>
```

```
<!DOCTYPE html>
<html>
<head>
    <meta chrset="UTF 8">
    <title>Event Registration</title>

</head>
<body>

<script src="https://code.angularjs.org/1.6.9/angular-route.js">
</script>
<script src="https://code.angularjs.org/1.6.9/angular.min.js">
</script>

<h1> Guru99 Global Event</h1>

<div ng-app="" ng-init="person={firstName:'Guru',lastName:'99'}">

       
    First Name : {{person.firstName}}<br>   
    Last Name : {{person.lastName}}

</div>

</body>
</html>
```

Code Explanation:

1. The ng-init directive is used to define the object person which in turn has key value pairs of firstName with the value "Guru" and the variable lastName with the value of "99".
2. We are then using expressions of {{person.firstName}} and {{person.secondName}} to access the value of these variables and display them in the view accordingly. Since the actual member variables are part of the object person, they have to access it with the dot (.) notation to access their actual value.

If the code is executed successfully, the following Output will be shown when you run your code in the browser.

Output:

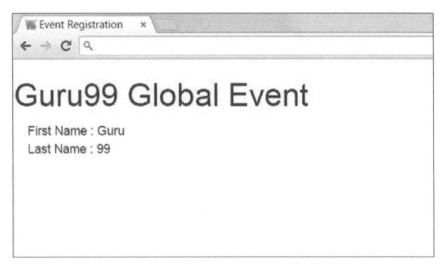

From the output,

- It can be clearly seen that the values of "firstName" and "secondName" are displayed on the screen.

AngularJS Arrays

Expressions can be used to work with arrays as well. Let's look at an example of Angular JS expressions with arrays.

In this example, we are going to define an array which is going to hold the marks of a student in 3 subjects. In the view, we will display the value of these marks accordingly.

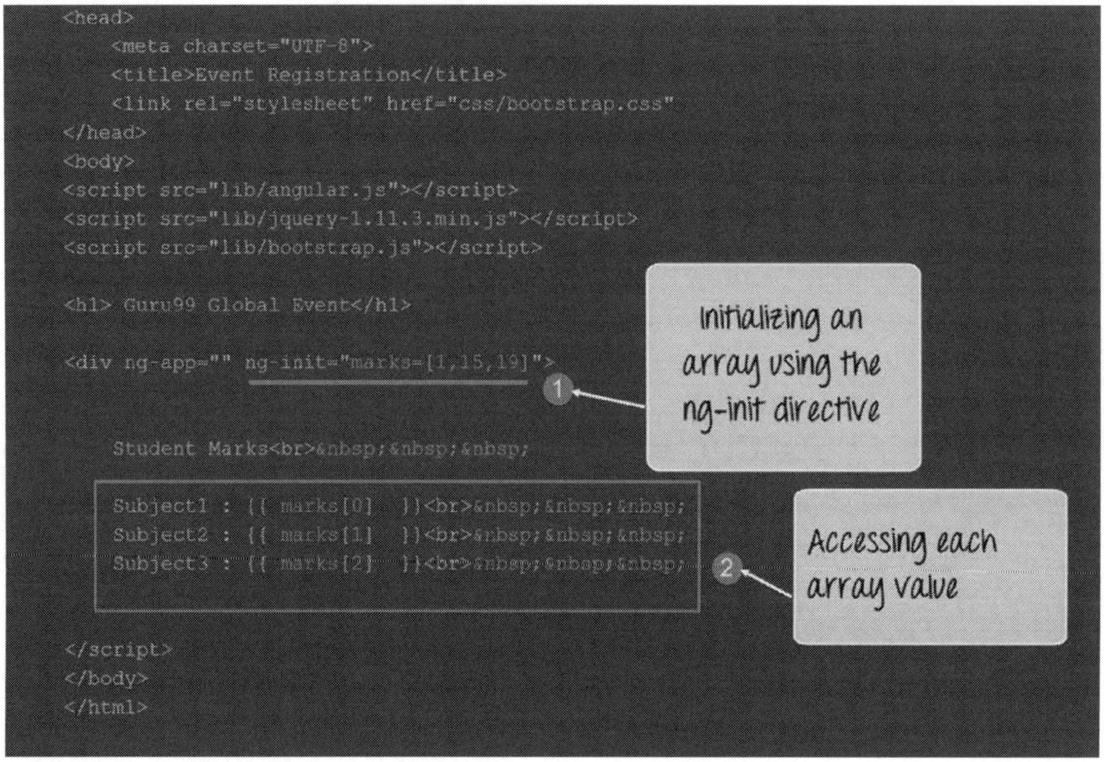

```html
<!DOCTYPE html>
<html>
<head>
    <meta chrset="UTF 8">
    <title>Event Registration</title>
</head>
<body>

<script src="https://code.angularjs.org/1.6.9/angular-route.js">
</script>
<script src="https://code.angularjs.org/1.6.9/angular.min.js">
</script>

<h1> Guru99 Global Event</h1>

<div ng-app="" ng-init="marks=[1,15,19]">

    Student Marks<br>   
    Subject1 : {{marks[0] }}<br>   
    Subject2 : {{marks[1] }}<br>   
    Subject3 : {{marks[2] }}<br>   
</div>

</body>
```

```
</html>
```

Code Explanation:

1. The ng-init directive is used define the array with the name "marks" with 3 values of 1, 15 and 19.
2. We are then using expressions of marks [index] to access each element of the array.

If the code is executed successfully, the following Output will be shown when you run your code in the browser.

Output:

From the output, it can be clearly seen that the marks being displayed, that are defined in the array.

AngularJS Expression capabilities and Limitations

Angular.JS Expression capabilities

1. Angular expressions are like JavaScript expressions. Hence, it has the same power and flexibility.
2. In JavaScript, when you try to evaluate undefined properties, it generates a ReferenceError or TypeError. In Angular, expression evaluation is forgiving and generate an undefined or null.
3. One can use filters within expressions to format data before

displaying it.

Angular JS Expression limitations

1. There is currently no availability to use conditionals, loops, or exceptions in an Angular expression
2. You cannot declare functions in an Angular expression, even inside ng-init directive.
3. One cannot create regular expressions in an Angular expression. A regular expression is a combination of symbols and characters, which are used to find for strings such as .*.txt$. Such expressions cannot be used within Angular JS expressions.
4. Also, one cannot use, or void in an Angular expression.

Difference between expression and $eval

The $eval function allows one to evaluate expressions from within the controller itself. So while expressions are used for evaluation in the view, the $eval is used in the controller function.

Let's look at a simple example on this.

In this example,

We are just going to use the $eval function to add 2 numbers and make it available in the scope object so that it can be shown in the view.

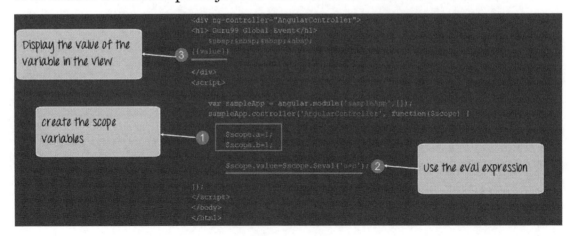

```
<!DOCTYPE html>
<html>
<head>
    <meta chrset="UTF 8">
    <title>Event Registration</title>
</head>
<body>

<script src="https://code.angularjs.org/1.6.9/angular-route.js">
</script>
<script src="https://code.angularjs.org/1.6.9/angular.min.js">
</script>
<script src="https://code.jquery.com/jquery-3.3.1.min.js">
</script>

<div ng-controller="AngularController">
    <h1> Guru99 Global Event</h1>
        
    {{value}}
</div>
<script>
    var sampleApp = angular.module('sampleApp',[]);
    sampleApp.controller('AngularController',function($scope){
        $scope.a=1;
        $scope.b=1;

        $scope.value=$scope.$eval('a+b');
    });
</script>

</body>
</html>
```

Code Explanation:

1. We are first defining 2 variables 'a' and 'b', each holding a value of 1.
2. We are using the $scope.$eval function to evaluate the addition of the 2 variables and assigning it to the scope variable 'value'.
3. We are then just displaying the value of the variable 'value' in the view.

If the code is executed successfully, the following Output will be shown when you run your code in the browser.

Output:

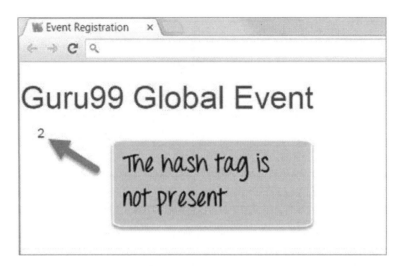

The above output shows the output of the expression which was evaluated in the controller. The above results show that the $eval expression was used to perform the addition of the 2 scope variables 'a and b' with the result sent and displayed in the view.

Summary:

- We have seen how expressions in Angular JS can be used to evaluate regular JavaScript like expressions such as the simple addition of numbers.
- The ng-init directive can be used to define variables in-line which can be used in the view.
- Expressions can be made to work with primitive types such as strings and numbers.
- Expressions can also be used to work with other types such as JavaScript objects and arrays.
- Expressions in Angular JS does have a few limitations like for example not being to have regular expressions or use functions, loops or conditional statements.

Chapter 9: Filter

What is Filter in AngularJS?

A filter formats the value of an expression to display to the user.

For example, if you want to have your strings in either in lowercase or all in uppercase, you can do this by using filters in Angular.

There are built-in filters such as 'lowercase', 'uppercase' which can retrieve the output in lowercase and uppercase accordingly. Similarly, for numbers, you can use other filters.

During this tutorial, we will see the different standard built-in filters available in Angular.

Lowercase

This filter takes on a string output and formats the string and displays all the characters in the string as lowercase.

Let's look at an example of AngularJS filters with the lowercase option.

In the below example, we will use a controller to send a string to a view via the scope object. We will then use a filter in the view to convert the string to lowercase.

```
<body>
<script src="lib/angular.js"></script>
<script src="lib/bootstrap.js"></script>
<script src="lib/jquery-2.1.4.min.js"></script>
<h1>Gur99 Global Event</h1>
<div ng-app="DemoApp" ng-controller="DemoController">
    Tutorial Name : <input type="text" ng-model="tutorialName"><br>
    <br>
    This tutorial is {{tutorialName | lowercase}}
</div>
<script type="text/javascript">
    var app = angular.module('DemoApp', []);
    app.controller('DemoController', function($scope) {
        $scope.tutorialName = "Angular JS";
    });
</script>
</body>
</html>
```

② Usage of the lower case filter.

① We are passing a string with a combination of uppercase and lowercase characters.

```
<!DOCTYPE html>
<html>
<head>
    <meta chrset="UTF 8">
    <title>Event Registration</title>
</head>
<body>

<script src="https://code.angularjs.org/1.6.9/angular-route.js">
</script>
<script src="https://code.angularjs.org/1.6.9/angular.min.js">
</script>
<script src="https://code.jquery.com/jquery-3.3.1.min.js">
</script>

    <h1> Guru99 Global Event</h1>
<div ng-app="DemoApp" ng-controller="DemoController">
    Tutorial Name : <input type="text" ng-model="tutorialName">
<br>
    <br>
    This tutorial is {{tutorialName | lowercase}}

</div>
<script type="text/javascript">
    var app = angular.module('DemoApp',[]);
    app.controller('DemoController',function($scope){

        $scope.tutorialName ="Angular JS";
    });
</script>
```

```
</body>
</html>
```

Code Explanation:

1. Here we are passing a string, which is a combination of lowercase and uppercase characters in a member variable called "tutorialName" and attaching it to the scope object. The value of the string being passed is "AngularJS".
2. We are using the member variable "tutorialName" and putting a filter symbol (|) which means that the output needs to be modified by using a filter. We then use the lowercase keyword to say to use the built-in filter to output the entire string in lowercase.

If the code is executed successfully, the following Output will be shown when you run your code in the browser.

Output:

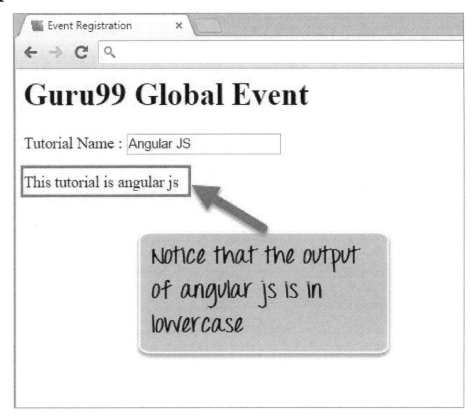

From the output

- It can be seen that the string "AngularJS" which was passed in the variable tutorialName which was a combination of lowercase and uppercase characters has been executed.
- After execution, the final output is in lowercase as shown above.

Uppercase

This filter is similar to the lowercase filter; the difference is that takes on a string output and formats the string and displays all the characters in the string as uppercase.

Let's look at an example of Angular JS filters with the lowercase option.

In the below example we will use a controller to send a string to a view via the scope object. We will then use a filter in the view to convert the string to uppercase.

```
<body>
<script src="lib/angular.js"></script>
<script src="lib/bootstrap.js"></script>
<script src="lib/jquery-2.1.4.min.js"></script>
<h1>Gur99 Global Event</h1>
<div ng-app="DemoApp" ng-controller="DemoController">
    Tutorial Name : <input type="text" ng-model="tutorialName"><br>
    <br>
    This tutorial is {{tutorialName | uppercase}}
</div>
<script type="text/javascript">
    var app = angular.module('DemoApp', []);
    app.controller('DemoController', function($scope) {
        $scope.tutorialName = "Angular JS";
    });
</script>
</body>
</html>
```

② Usage of the upper case filter.

① We are passing a string with a combination of uppercase and lowercase characters.

```
<!DOCTYPE html>
<html>
<head>
    <meta chrset="UTF 8">
    <title>Event Registration</title>
```

```
</head>
<body>

<script src="https://code.angularjs.org/1.6.9/angular-route.js">
</script>
<script src="https://code.angularjs.org/1.6.9/angular.min.js">
</script>
<script src="https://code.jquery.com/jquery-3.3.1.min.js">
</script>

    <h1> Guru99 Global Event</h1>
<div ng-app="DemoApp" ng-controller="DemoController">
    Tutorial Name : <input type="text" ng-model="tutorialName">
<br>
    <br>
    This tutorial is {{tutorialName | uppercase}}

</div>
<script type="text/javascript">
    var app = angular.module('DemoApp',[]);
    app.controller('DemoController',function($scope){

        $scope.tutorialName ="Angular JS";
    });
</script>

</body>
</html>
```

Code Explanation:

1. Here we are passing a string which is a combination of lowercase and uppercase characters "Angular JS" in a member variable called "tutorialName" and attaching it to the scope object.
2. We are using the member variable "tutorialName" and putting a filter symbol (|), which means that the output needs to be modified by using a filter. We then use the uppercase keyword to say to use the built-in filter to output the entire string in uppercase.

If the code is executed successfully, the following Output will be shown when you run your code in the browser.

Output:

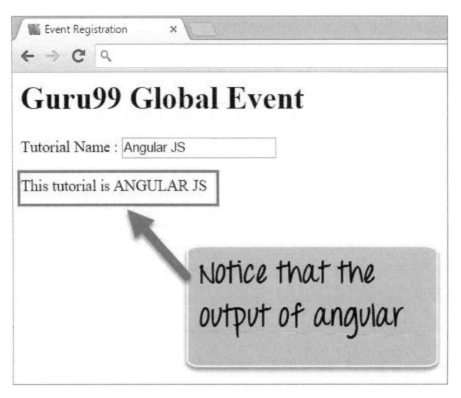

From the output,

- It can be seen that the string which was passed in the variable tutorialName which was a combination of lowercase and uppercase characters has been outputted in all uppercase.

Number

This filter formats a number and can apply a limit to the decimal points for a number.

Let's look at an example of AngularJS filters with the number option.

In the example below,

We wanted to showcase how we can use the number filter to format a number to display with a restriction of 2 decimal places.

We will use a controller to send a number to a view via the scope object. We will then use a filter in the view to apply the number filter.

```
<body>
<script src="lib/angular.js"></script>
<script src="lib/bootstrap.js"></script>
<script src="lib/jquery-2.1.4.min.js"></script>
<h1>Guru99 Global Event</h1>
<div ng-app="DemoApp" ng-controller="DemoController">
        This tutorialID is {{tutorialID | number:2}}
</div>
<script type="text/javascript">
    var app = angular.module('DemoApp', []);
    app.controller('DemoController', function($scope) {
        $scope.tutorialID = 3.565656;
    });
</script>
</body>
</html>
```

② Using the number filter

① Passing a decimal number with a more number of decimal points

```
<!DOCTYPE html>
<html>
<head>
    <meta chrset="UTF 8">
    <title>Event Registration</title>
</head>
<body>

<script src="https://code.angularjs.org/1.6.9/angular-route.js">
</script>
<script src="https://code.angularjs.org/1.6.9/angular.min.js">
</script>
<script src="https://code.jquery.com/jquery-3.3.1.min.js">
</script>

<h1> Guru99 Global Event</h1>
<div ng-app="DemoApp" ng-controller="DemoController">

    This tutorialID is {{tutorialID | number:2}}

</div>
<script type="text/javascript">
    var app = angular.module('DemoApp',[]);
    app.controller('DemoController',function($scope){

        $scope.tutorialID =3.565656;
    });
</script>

</body>
</html>
```

Code Explanation:

1. Here we are passing a number with a larger number of decimal places in a member variable called tutorialID and attaching it to the scope object.
2. We are using the member variable tutorialID and putting a filter symbol (|) along with the number filter. Now in number:2, the two indicates that the filter should restrict the number of decimal places to 2.

If the code is executed successfully, the following Output will be shown when you run your code in the browser.

Output:

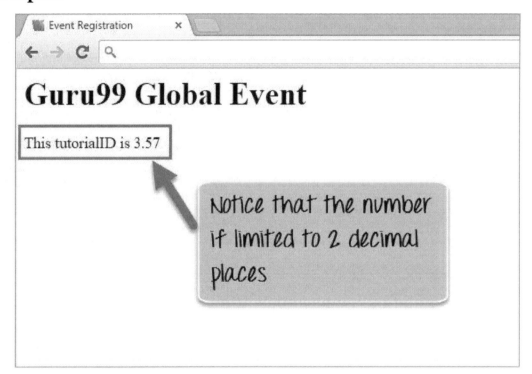

From the output,

- It can be seen that the number which was passed in the variable tutorialID which had a large number of decimal points has been limited to 2 decimal places because of the number: 2 filters which was applied.

Currency

This filter formats a currency filter to a number.

Suppose, if you wanted to display a number with a currency such as $, then this filter can be used.

In the below example we will use a controller to send a number to a view via the scope object. We will then use a filter in the view to apply the current filter.

```
<body>
<script src="lib/angular.js"></script>
<script src="lib/bootstrap.js"></script>
<script src="lib/jquery-2.1.4.min.js"></script>
<h1>Guru99 Global Event</h1>
<div ng-app="DemoApp" ng-controller="DemoController">
        This tutorialID is {{tutorialprice | currency}}
</div>
<script type="text/javascript">
    var app = angular.module('DemoApp', []);
    app.controller("DemoController", function($scope) {
        $scope.tutorialprice = 20.56;
    });
</script>
</body>
</html>
```

Applying the currency ②

① Passing a decimal number in the scope object.

```
<!DOCTYPE html>
<html>
<head>
    <meta chrset="UTF 8">
    <title>Event Registration</title>
</head>
<body>

<script src="https://code.angularjs.org/1.6.9/angular-route.js">
</script>
<script src="https://code.angularjs.org/1.6.9/angular.min.js">
</script>
<script src="https://code.jquery.com/jquery-3.3.1.min.js">
</script>

<h1> Guru99 Global Event</h1>
<div ng-app="DemoApp" ng-controller="DemoController">
```

```
    This tutorial Price is {{tutorialprice | currency}}

</div>
<script type="text/javascript">
    var app = angular.module('DemoApp',[]);
    app.controller('DemoController',function($scope){

        $scope.tutorialprice =20.56;
    });
</script>

</body>
</html>
```

Code Explanation:

1. Here we are passing a number in a member variable called tutorialprice and attaching it to the scope object.
2. We are using the member variable tutorialprice and putting a filter symbol (|) along with the currency filter. Note that the currency which is applied depends on the language settings which are applied to the machine.

If the code is executed successfully, the following Output will be shown when you run your code in the browser.

Output:

From the output

- It can be seen the currency symbol has been appended to the number which was passed in the variable tutorialprice.
- In our case, since the language settings are English (United States), the $ symbol is inserted as the currency.

JSON

This filter formats a JSON like input and applies the JSON filter to give the output in JSON.

In the below example we will use a controller to send a JSON type object to a view via the scope object. We will then use a filter in the view to apply the JSON filter.

```
<body>
<script src="lib/angular.js"></script>
<script src="lib/bootstrap.js"></script>
<script src="lib/jquery-2.1.4.min.js"></script>
<h1>Gur99 Global Event</h1>
<div ng-app="DemoApp" ng-controller="DemoController">
    This tutorial is {{tutorial | json}}
</div>
<script type="text/javascript">
    var app = angular.module('DemoApp', []);
    app.controller('DemoController', function($scope) {
        $scope.tutorial = {TutorialID:12,TutorialName:"Angular"}
    });
</script>
</body>
</html>
```

Applying the json filter. ②

① Passing a json type string in the scope object

```html
<!DOCTYPE html>
<html>
<head>
    <meta chrset="UTF 8">
    <title>Event Registration</title>
</head>
<body>

<script src="https://code.angularjs.org/1.6.9/angular-route.js">
</script>
<script src="https://code.angularjs.org/1.6.9/angular.min.js">
</script>
<script src="https://code.jquery.com/jquery-3.3.1.min.js">
</script>

<h1> Guru99 Global Event</h1>
<div ng-app="DemoApp" ng-controller="DemoController">

    This tutorial is {{tutorial | json}}

</div>
<script type="text/javascript">
    var app = angular.module('DemoApp',[]);
    app.controller('DemoController',function($scope){

        $scope.tutorial ={TutorialID:12,tutorialName:"Angular"};
    });
</script>

</body>
</html>
```

Code Explanation:

1. Here we are passing a number in a member variable called "tutorial" and attaching it to the scope object. This member variable contains a JSON type string of Tutorial ID:12, and TutorialName:"Angular".
2. We are using the member variable tutorial and putting a filter symbol (|) along with the JSON filter.

If the code is executed successfully, the following Output will be shown when you run your code in the browser.

Output:

From the output,

- It can be seen that the JSON like a string is parsed and displayed a proper JSON object in the browser.

Summary:

- Filters are used to change the way the output is displayed to the user.

- Angular provides built-in filters such as the lowercase and uppercase filters to change the output of strings to lower and uppercase respectively.
- There is also a provision for changing the way numbers are displayed by using the number filter by specifying the number of decimal points to be displayed in the number.
- One can also use the currency filter to append the currency symbol to any number.
- If there is a requirement to have json specific output, angular also provides the JSON filter for filtering any JSON like string into JSON format.

Chapter 10: Custom Filter

Sometimes the built-in filters in Angular cannot meet the needs or requirements for filtering output. In such a case a custom filter can be created which can pass the output in the required manner.

In the below example we are going to pass a string to the view from the controller via the scope object, but we don't want the string to be displayed as it is.

We want to ensure that whenever we display the string, we pass a custom filter which will append another string and displayed the completed string to the user.

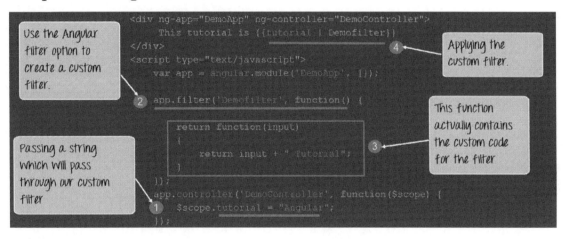

```
<!DOCTYPE html>
<html>
<head>
    <meta chrset="UTF 8">
    <title>Event Registration</title>
</head>
<body>

<script src="https://code.angularjs.org/1.6.9/angular-route.js">
</script>
<script src="https://code.angularjs.org/1.6.9/angular.min.js">
</script>
<script src="https://code.jquery.com/jquery-3.3.1.min.js">
</script>

<h1> Guru99 Global Event</h1>
```

```
<div ng-app="DemoApp" ng-controller="DemoController">

    This tutorial is {{tutorial | Demofilter}}

</div>
<script type="text/javascript">
    var app = angular.module('DemoApp',[]);
    app.filter('Demofilter',function(){
        return function(input)
        {
            return input + " Tutorial"
        }
    });

    app.controller('DemoController',function($scope){

        $scope.tutorial ="Angular";
    });

</script>

</body>
</html>
```

Code Explanation:

1. Here we are passing a string "Angular" in a member variable called tutorial and attaching it to the scope object.
2. Angular provides the filter service which can be used to create our custom filter. The 'Demofilter' is a name given to our filter.
3. This is the standard way in which a custom filter is defined wherein a function is returned. This function is what contains the custom code to create the custom filter. In our function, we are taking a string "Angular" which is passed from our view to the filter and appending the string "Tutorial" to this.
4. We are using our Demofilter on our member variable which was passed from the controller to the view.

If the code is executed successfully, the following Output will be shown when you run your code in the browser.

Output:

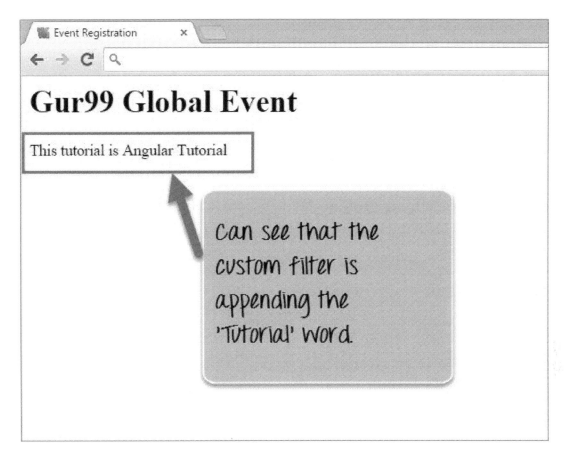

From the output,

- It can be seen that our custom filter has been applied and
- The word 'Tutorial' has been appended at the end of the string, which was passed in member variable tutorial.

Summary:

If there is a requirement that is not met by any of the filters defined in angular, then you can create your custom filter and add your custom code to determine the type of output you want from the filter.a

Chapter 11: Directive

What is an AngularJS directive?

A directive in AngularJS is a command that gives HTML new functionality. When angular go through the HTML code, it will first find the directives in the page and then parse the HTML page accordingly.

A simple example of an AngularJS directive, which we have seen in earlier chapters is the "ng-model directive". This directive is used to bind our data model to our view.

Note: You can have basic angular code in an HTML page with the ng-init, ng-repeat and ng-model directives without the need to have Controllers. The logic for these directives is in the Angular.js file which is provided by Google. Controllers are the next level angular programming constructs that allow business logic, but as mentioned for an application to be an angular application it's not mandatory to have a controller.

How to Create Directive

As we defined in the introduction, AngularJS directives is a way to extend the functionality of HTML.

There are 4 directives defined in AngularJS.

Below is the list of the AngularJS directives along with examples provided to explain each one of them.

1) ng-app

This is used to initialize an Angular.JS application. When this directive in place in an HTML page, it basically tells Angular that this HTML page is an angular.js application.

The example below shows how to use the ng-app directive. In this example, we are simply going to show how to make a normal HTML application an angularJS application.

```html
<!DOCTYPE html>
<html>
<head>
    <meta charset="UTF-8">
    <title>Event Registration</title>
    <link rel="stylesheet" href="css/bootstrap.css"
</head>
<script src="lib/angular.js"></script>
<script src="lib/angular-route.js"></script>

<script src="lib/jquery-1.11.3.min.js"></script>
<script src="lib/bootstrap.js"></script>

<h1> Guru99 Global Event</h1>

<div ng-app="">        ①

    Tutorial Name : {{ "Angular" + "JS"}}

</div>        ②

</script>
</body>
</html>
```

① Defining the application as an angular application via the ng-app directive

② Making use of Angular JS expressions

```html
<!DOCTYPE html>
<html>
<head>
    <meta chrset="UTF 8">
    <title>Event Registration</title>
</head>
<body>

<script src="https://code.angularjs.org/1.6.9/angular-route.js">
</script>
<script src="https://code.angularjs.org/1.6.9/angular.js">
</script>
<script src="https://code.angularjs.org/1.6.9/angular.min.js">
</script>
```

```
<script src="https://code.jquery.com/jquery-3.3.1.min.js">
</script>

<h1> Guru99 Global Event</h1>

<div ng-app="">

    Tutorial Name : {{ "Angular" + "JS"}}

</div>

</body>
</html>
```

Code Explanation:

1. The "ng-app" directive is added to our div tag to indicate that this application is an angular.js application. Note that the ng-app directive can be applied to any tag, so it can also be put in the body tag as well.
2. Because we have defined this application as an angular.js application, we can now make use of the angular.js functionality. In our case, we are using expressions to simply concatenate 2 strings.

If the code is executed successfully, the following Output will be shown when you run your code in the browser.

Output:

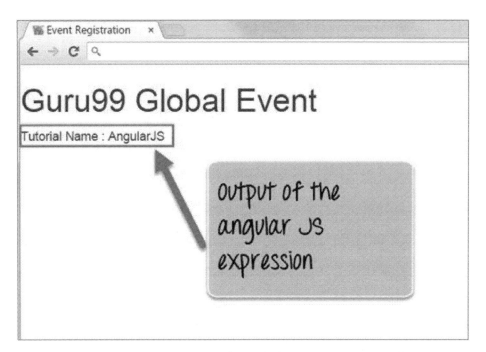

The output clearly shows the output of the expression which was only made possible because we defined the application as an angularjs application.

2) ng-init

This is used to initialize application data. Sometimes you may require some local data for your application, this can be done with the ng-init directive.

The example below shows how to use the ng-init directive.

In this example, we are going to create a variable called "TutorialName" using the ng-init directive and display the value of that variable on the page.

```
<!DOCTYPE html>
<html>
<head>
    <meta charset="UTF-8">
    <title>Event Registration</title>
    <link rel="stylesheet" href="css/bootstrap.css"
</head>
<script src="lib/angular.js"></script>
<script src="lib/angular-route.js"></script>

<script src="lib/jquery-1.11.3.min.js"></script>
<script src="lib/bootstrap.js"></script>

<h1> Guru99 Global Event</h1>

<div ng-app="" ng-init="TutorialName='Angular JS'">

    Tutorial Name : {{ TutorialName}}

</div>

</script>
</body>
</html>
```

using the ng-init directive to define a local variable

①

using the local variable in the expression.

②

```
<!DOCTYPE html>
<html>
<head>
    <meta chrset="UTF 8">
    <title>Event Registration</title>
</head>
<body>

<script src="https://code.angularjs.org/1.6.9/angular-route.js">
</script>
<script src="https://code.angularjs.org/1.6.9/angular.js">
</script>
<script src="https://code.angularjs.org/1.6.9/angular.min.js">
</script>
<script src="https://code.jquery.com/jquery-3.3.1.min.js">
</script>

<h1> Guru99 Global Event</h1>

<div ng-app="" ng-init="TutorialName='Angular JS'">

    Tutorial Name : {{ TutorialName}}

</div>

</body>
```

```
</html>
```

Code Explanation:

1. The ng-init directive is added to our div tag to define a local variable called "TutorialName" and the value given to this is "AngularJS".
2. We are using expressions in AngularJs to display the output of the variable name "TutorialName" which was defined in our ng-init directive.

If the code is executed successfully, the following Output will be shown when you run your code in the browser.

Output:

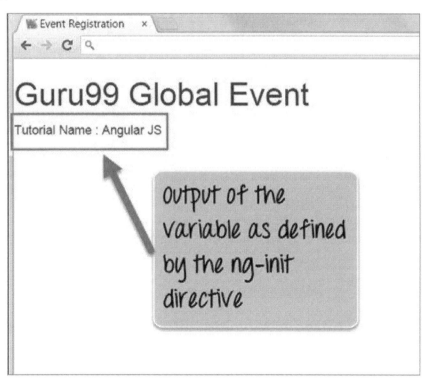

In the output,

- The result clearly shows the output of the expression which contains the string "AngularJS". This is as a result of the string "AngularJS" being assigned to the variable 'TutorialName' in the ng-init section.

3) ng-model

And finally, we have the ng-model directive, which is used to bind the value of an HTML control to application data. The example below shows how to use the ng-model directive.

In this example,

- We are going to create 2 variables called "quantity" and "price". These variables are going to be bound to 2 text input controls.
- We are then going to display the total amount based on the multiplication of both price and quantity values.

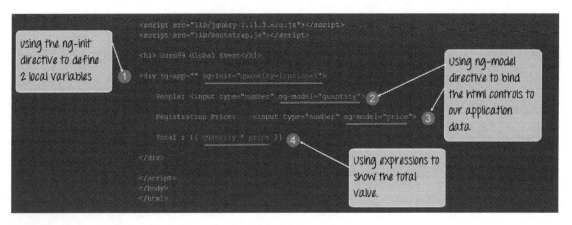

```
<!DOCTYPE html>
<html>
<head>
    <meta chrset="UTF 8">
    <title>Event Registration</title>
</head>
<body>

<script src="https://code.angularjs.org/1.6.9/angular-route.js">
</script>
<script src="https://code.angularjs.org/1.6.9/angular.js">
</script>
<script src="https://code.angularjs.org/1.6.9/angular.min.js">
</script>
<script src="https://code.jquery.com/jquery-3.3.1.min.js">
</script>

<h1> Guru99 Global Event</h1>
```

```
<div ng-app="" ng-init="quantity=1;price=5">

    People : <input type="number" ng-model="quantity">

    Registration Price : <input type="number" ng-model="price">

    Total : {{quantity * price}}
</div>

</body>
</html>
```

Code Explanation:

1. The ng-init directive is added to our div tag to define 2 local variables; one is called "quantity" and the other is "price".
2. Now we are using the ng-model directive to bind the text boxes of "People" and "Registration price" to our local variables "quantity" and "price" respectively.
3. Finally, we are showing the Total via an expression, which is the multiplication of the quantity and price variables.

If the code is executed successfully, the following Output will be shown when you run your code in the browser.

Output:

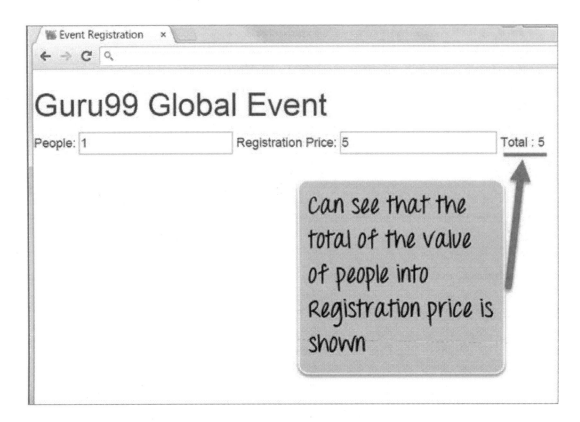

- The output clearly shows the multiplication of the values for People and Registration price.

Now, if you go to the text boxes and change the value of the People and Registration price, the Total will automatically change.

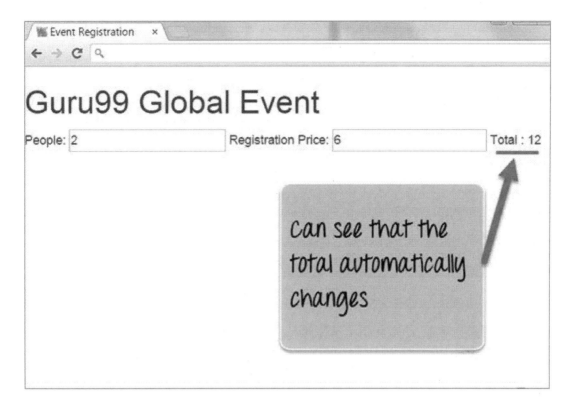

- The above output just shows the power of data binding in
  angularJs, which is achieved with the use of the ng-model
  directive.

4) ng-repeat

This is used to repeat an HTML element. The example below shows
how to use the ng-repeat directive.

In this example,

- We are going to have an array of chapter names in an array
  variable and
- then use the ng-repeat directive to display each element of the
  array as a list item

```
</head>
<script src="lib/angular.js"></script>
<script src="lib/angular-route.js"></script>

<script src="lib/jquery-1.11.3.min.js"></script>
<script src="lib/bootstrap.js"></script>

<h1> Guru99 Global Event</h1>

<div ng-app="" ng-init="chapters=['Controllers','Models','Filters']">
    <ul>

        <li ng-repeat="names in chapters">    ②
            {{ names }}  ③
        </li>
    </ul>
</div>

</div>

</script>
</body>
</html>
```

① We are defining an array called chapters.

② For each string in the chapters array, we are using the ng-repeat directive

③ Using expressions to show each name in the chapters array variable.

```html
<!DOCTYPE html>
<html>
<head>
    <meta chrset="UTF 8">
    <title>Event Registration</title>
</head>
<body>

<script src="https://code.angularjs.org/1.6.9/angular-route.js">
</script>
<script src="https://code.angularjs.org/1.6.9/angular.js">
</script>
<script src="https://code.angularjs.org/1.6.9/angular.min.js">
</script>
<script src="https://code.jquery.com/jquery-3.3.1.min.js">
</script>

<h1> Guru99 Global Event</h1>

<div ng-app="" ng-init="chapters=
['Controllers','Models','Filters']">
    <ul>
        <li ng-repeat="names in chapters">
            {{names}}
        </li>
    </ul>

</div>

</body>
```

```
</html>
```

Code Explanation:

1. The ng-init directive is added to our div tag to define a variable called "chapters" which is an array variable containing 3 strings.
2. The ng-repeat element is used by declaring an inline variable called "names" and going through each element in the chapters array.
3. Finally, we are showing the value of the local inline variable 'names.'

If the code is executed successfully, the following Output will be shown when you run your code in the browser.

Output:

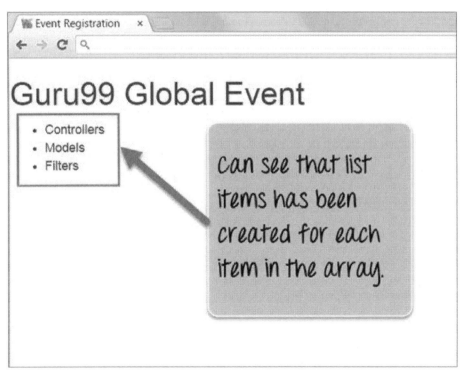

- The above output just shows that the ng-repeat directive took each value in the array called "chapters" and created HTML list items for each item in the array.

Summary

- Directives are used to extend the functionality of HTML. Angular provides inbuilt directives such as
  - ng-app – This is used to initialize an angular application.
  - ng-int – This is used to create application variables
  - ng-model – This is used to bind HTML controls to application data
  - ng-repeat – Used to repeat elements using angular.

Chapter 12: CUSTOM Directive

What is Custom Directive?

A custom directive in Angular Js is a user-defined directive with your desired functionality. Even though AngularJS has a lot of powerful directives out of the box, sometime custom directives are required.

How to Create a Custom Directive?

Let's take a look at an example of how we can create a custom directive.

The custom directive in our case is simply going to inject a div tag which has the text "AngularJS Tutorial" in our page when the directive is called.

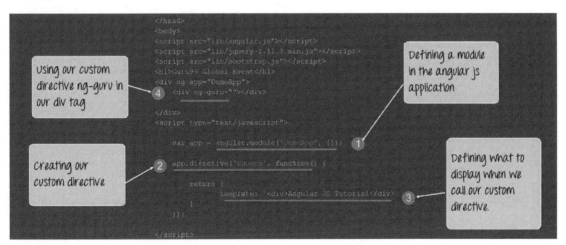

```
<!DOCTYPE html>
<html>
<head>
    <meta chrset="UTF 8">
    <title>Event Registration</title>
</head>
<body>
```

```html
<script src="https://code.angularjs.org/1.6.9/angular-route.js">
</script>
<script src="https://code.angularjs.org/1.6.9/angular.js">
</script>
<script src="https://code.angularjs.org/1.6.9/angular.min.js">
</script>
<script src="https://code.jquery.com/jquery-3.3.1.min.js">
</script>

<h1> Guru99 Global Event</h1>

<div ng-app="DemoApp">
    <div ng-guru=""></div>

</div>

<script type="text/javascript">
    var app = angular.module('DemoApp',[]);
    app.directive('ngGuru',function(){

    return {
        template: '<div>Angular JS Tutorial</div>'
    }
    });

</script>

</body>
</html>
```

Code Explanation:

1. We are first creating a module for our angular application. This is required to create a custom directive because the directive will be created using this module.
2. We are now creating a custom directive called "ngGuru" and defining a function which will have custom code for our directive.

Note:-

Note that when defining the directive, we have defined it as ngGuru with the letter 'G' as capital. And when we access it from our div tag as a directive we are accessing it as ng-guru. This is how angular understands custom directives defined in an application. Firstly the name of the custom directive should start with the letters 'ng'. Secondly the hyphen symbol '-' should only be mentioned when calling the directive. And thirdly the first letter following the letters 'ng' when defining the directive can be either lower or uppercase.

3. We are using the template parameter which a parameter defined by Angular for custom directives. In this, we are defining that whenever this directive is used, then just use the value of the template and inject it in the calling code.

4. Here we are now making use of our custom created "ng-guru" directive. When we do this, the value we defined for our template "<div>Angular JS Tutorial</div>" will now be injected here.

If the code is executed successfully, the following Output will be shown when you run your code in the browser.

Output:

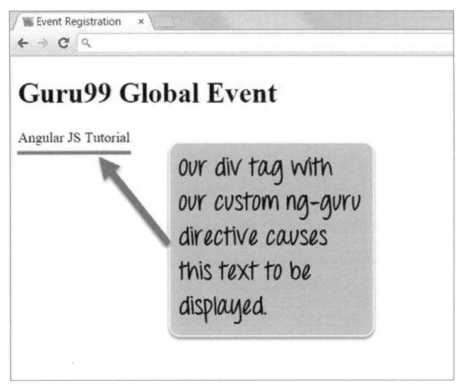

- The above output clearly shows that our custom ng-guru directive, which has the template defined for showing a custom text gets displayed in the browser.

AngularJs Directives and Scopes

The scope is defined as the glue which binds the controller to the view by managing the data between the view and the controller.

When creating custom AngularJs directives, they by default will have access to the scope object in the parent controller.

In this way, it becomes easy for the custom directive to make use of the data being passed to the main controller.

Let's look at an example of how we can use the scope of a parent controller in our custom directive.

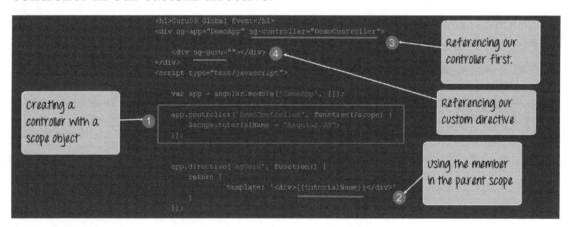

```html
<!DOCTYPE html>
<html>
<head>
    <meta chrset="UTF 8">
    <title>Event Registration</title>
</head>
<body>

<script src="https://code.angularjs.org/1.6.9/angular-route.js">
</script>
<script src="https://code.angularjs.org/1.6.9/angular.js">
</script>
<script src="https://code.angularjs.org/1.6.9/angular.min.js">
</script>
<script src="https://code.jquery.com/jquery-3.3.1.min.js">
</script>
```

```
<h1> Guru99 Global Event</h1>

<div ng-app="DemoApp" ng-controller="DemoController">
    <div ng-guru=""></div>

</div>

<script type="text/javascript">

    var app = angular.module('DemoApp',[]);

    app.controller('DemoController',function($scope) {
        $scope.tutorialName = "Angular JS";

    });

        app.directive('ngGuru',function(){
        return {
         template: '<div>{{tutorialName}}</div>'
    }
    });

</script>

</body>
</html>
```

Code Explanation:

1. We first create a controller called, "DemoController". In this, we defining a variable called tutorialName and attaching it to the scope object in one statement - $scope.tutorialName = "AngularJS".

2. In our custom directive, we can call the variable "tutorialName" by using an expression. This variable would be accessible because it is defined in the controller "DemoController", which would become the parent for this directive.

3. We reference the controller in a div tag, which will act as our parent div tag. Note that this needs to be done first in order for our custom directive to access the tutorialName variable.

4. We finally just attach our custom directive "ng-guru" to our div tag.

If the code is executed successfully, the following Output will be shown when you run your code in the browser.

Output:

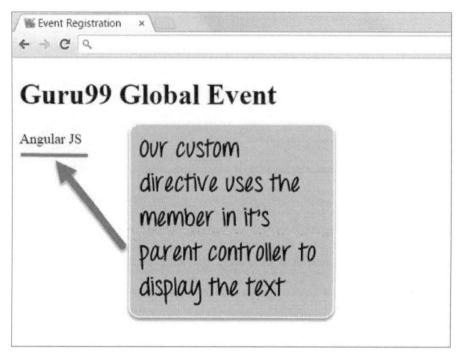

- The above output clearly shows that our custom directive "ng-guru" makes use of the scope variable tutorialName in the parent controller.

Using controllers with directives

Angular gives the facility to **access the controller's member variable directly from custom directives** without the need of the scope object.

This becomes necessary at times because in an application you may have multiple scope objects belonging to multiple controllers.

So there is a high chance that you could make the mistake of accessing the scope object of the wrong controller.

In such scenario's there is a way to specifically mention saying "I want to access this specific controller" from my directive.

Let's take a look at an example of how we can achieve this.

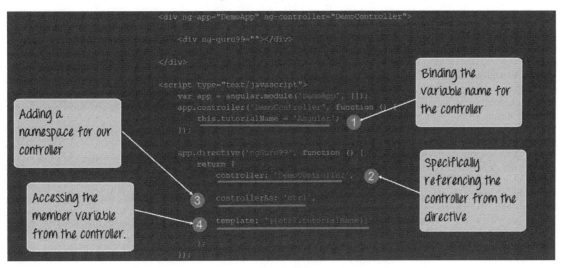

```html
<!DOCTYPE html>
<html>
<head>
    <meta chrset="UTF 8">
    <title>Event Registration</title>
</head>
<body>

<script src="https://code.angularjs.org/1.6.9/angular-route.js">
</script>
<script src="https://code.angularjs.org/1.6.9/angular.js">
</script>
<script src="https://code.angularjs.org/1.6.9/angular.min.js">
</script>
<script src="https://code.jquery.com/jquery-3.3.1.min.js">
</script>

<h1> Guru99 Global Event</h1>

<div ng-app="DemoApp" ng-controller="DemoController">
    <div ng-guru99=""></div>

</div>

<script type="text/javascript">

    var app = angular.module('DemoApp',[]);

    app.controller('DemoController',function() {
        this.tutorialName = "Angular";

    });
```

```
      app.directive('ngGuru99',function(){
          return {
          controller: 'DemoController',

            controllerAs: 'ctrl',

            template: '{{ctrl.tutorialName}}'
        };
      });

</script>

</body>
</html>
```

Code Explanation:

1. We first create a controller called, "DemoController". In this we
    will define a variable called "tutorialName" and this time instead
    of attaching it to the scope object, we will attach it directly to the
    controller.
2. In our custom directive, we are specifically mentioning that we
    want to use the controller "DemoController" by using the
    controller parameter keyword.
3. We create a reference to the controller using the "controllerAs"
    parameter. This is defined by Angular and is the way to reference
    the controller as a reference.

    Note: -It is possible to access multiple controllers in a directive by
    specifying respective blocks of the controller, controllerAs and
    template statements.

4. Finally, in our template, we are using the reference created in step
    3 and using the member variable that was attached directly to the
    controller in Step 1.

If the code is executed successfully, the following Output will be shown
when you run your code in the browser.

Output:

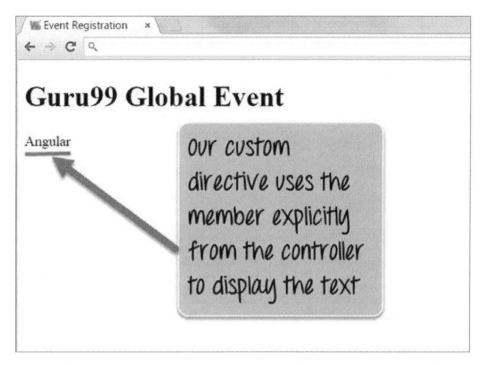

The output clearly shows that the custom directive is especially accessing the DemoController and the member variable tutorialName attached to it and displays the text "Angular".

How to create reusable directives

We already saw the power of custom directives, but we can take that to the next level by building our own re-usable directives.

Let's say, for example, that we wanted to inject code that would always show the below HTML tags across multiple screens, which is basically just an input for the "Name" and "age" of the user.

To reuse this function on multiple screens without coding each time, we create a master control or directive in angular to hold these controls ("Name" and "age" of the user).

So now, instead of entering the same code for the below screen every time, we can actually embed this code in a directive and embed that directive at any point in time.

Let' see an example of how we can achieve this.

Name	[ ]
Age	[ ]

```
<script src="lib/angular.js"></script>
<script src="lib/jquery-1.11.3.min.js"></script>
<script src="lib/bootstrap.js"></script>
<h1>Guru99 Global Event</h1>
<div ng-app="DemoApp">
    <div ng-guru=""></div>

</div>
<script type="text/javascript">

    var app = angular.module('DemoApp', []);

    app.directive('ngGuru', function() {

        return {
            template: '  Name <input type="text"><br><br>   Age <input type="text">'
        }
    });

</script>
</body>
</html>
```

Adding custom code to the template in the directive

```
<!DOCTYPE html>
<html>
<head>
    <meta chrset="UTF 8">
    <title>Event Registration</title>
</head>
<body>

<script src="https://code.angularjs.org/1.6.9/angular-route.js">
</script>
<script src="https://code.angularjs.org/1.6.9/angular.js">
</script>
<script src="https://code.angularjs.org/1.6.9/angular.min.js">
</script>
<script src="https://code.jquery.com/jquery-3.3.1.min.js">
</script>

<h1> Guru99 Global Event</h1>

<div ng-app="DemoApp">
    <div ng-guru=""></div>

</div>

<script type="text/javascript">

    var app = angular.module('DemoApp',[]);
```

```
    app.directive('ngGuru',function(){
        return {

            template: '  Name <input type="text"><br>
<br>   Age<input type="text">'
        };
    });

</script>

</body>
</html>
```

Code Explanation:

1. In our code snippet for a custom directive, what changes is just the value which is given to the template parameter of our custom directive.

   Instead of a plan five tag or text, we are actually entering the entire fragment of 2 input controls for the "Name" and "age" which needs to be shown on our page.

If the code is executed successfully, the following Output will be shown when you run your code in the browser.

Output:

From the above output, we can see that the code snippet from the template of the custom directive gets added to the page.

AngularJS Directives and components - ng-transclude

As we mentioned quite earlier, Angular is meant to extend the functionality of HTML. And we have already seen how we can have code injection by using custom re-usable directives.

But in the modern web application development, there is also a concept of developing web components. Which basically means creating our own HTML tags that can be used as components in our code.

Hence angular provides another level of power to extending HTML tags by giving the ability to inject attributes into the HTML tags itself.

This is done by the "**ng-transclude**" tag, which is a kind of setting to tell angular to capture everything that is put inside the directive in the markup.

Let's take an example of how we can achieve this.

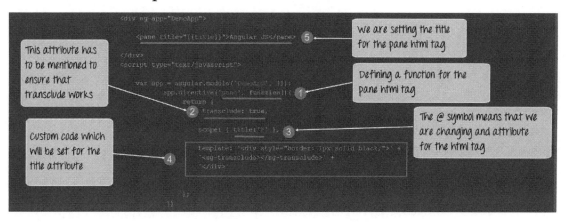

```
<!DOCTYPE html>
<html>
<head>
    <meta chrset="UTF 8">
    <title>Event Registration</title>
</head>
<body>

<script src="https://code.angularjs.org/1.6.9/angular-route.js">
</script>
<script src="https://code.angularjs.org/1.6.9/angular.js">
</script>
<script src="https://code.angularjs.org/1.6.9/angular.min.js">
</script>
<script src="https://code.jquery.com/jquery-3.3.1.min.js">
</script>

<h1> Guru99 Global Event</h1>

<div ng-app="DemoApp">
    <pane title="{{title}}">Angular JS</pane>

</div>

<script type="text/javascript">

    var app = angular.module('DemoApp',[]);

    app.directive('pane',function(){
        return {

            transclude:true,
            scope :{title:'@'},
            template: '<div style="border: 1px solid black;"> '+
```

```
                              '<ng-transclude></ng-transclude>'+
                              '</div>'
                };
            });

</script>

</body>
</html>
```

Code Explanation:

1. We are using the directive to define a custom HTML tag called 'pane' and adding a function which will put some custom code for this tag. In the output, our custom pane tag is going to display the text "AngularJS" in a rectangle with a solid black border.

2. The "transclude" attribute has to be mentioned as true, which is required by angular to inject this tag into our DOM.

3. In the scope, we are defining a title attribute. Attributes are normally defined as name/value pairs like: name="value". In our case, the name of the attribute in our pane HTML tag is "title". The "@" symbol is the requirement from angular. This is done so that when the line title={{title}} is executed in Step 5, the custom code for the title attribute gets added to the pane HTML tag.

4. The custom code for the title attributes which just draws a solid black border for our control.

5. Finally, we are calling our custom HTML tag along with the title attribute which was defined.

If the code is executed successfully, the following Output will be shown when you run your code in the browser.

Output:

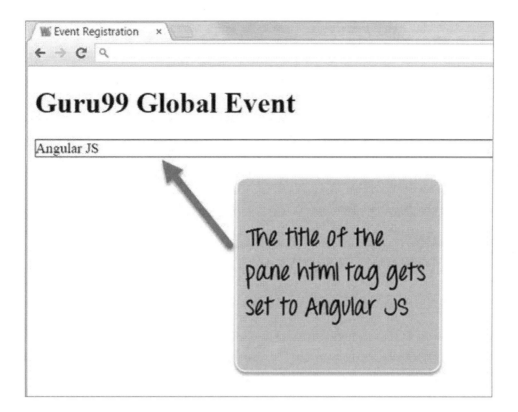

- The output clearly shows that the title attribute of the pane html5 tag has been set to the custom value of "Angular.JS".

Nested directives

Directives in angular can be nested. Like just inner modules or functions in any programming language, you may need to embed directives within each other.

You can get a better understanding of this by seeing the below example.

In this example, we are creating 2 directives called "outer" and "inner".

- The inner directive displays a text called "Inner".
- While the outer directive actually makes a call to the inner directive to display the text called "Inner".

Creating a outer directive

Required so that the outer directive can call the inner directive

Creating a inner nested directive.

Calling the outer directive

Calling the inner directive

```
<div ng-app="DemoApp">
    <outer></outer></div>

<script type="text/javascript">
var app = angular.module('DemoApp',[]);
app.directive('outer',function(){
    return {
        restrict:'E',
        template:'<div><h1>Outer</h1><inner></inner></div>',
    }});
app.directive('inner',function(){
    return {
        restrict:'E',
        template:'<div><h1>Inner</h1></div>',
    }
    });
</script>
```

```
</head>
<body>

<script src="https://code.angularjs.org/1.6.9/angular-route.js">
</script>
<script src="https://code.angularjs.org/1.6.9/angular.js">
</script>
<script src="https://code.angularjs.org/1.6.9/angular.min.js">
</script>
<script src="https://code.jquery.com/jquery-3.3.1.min.js">
</script>

<h1> Guru99 Global Event</h1>

<div ng-app="DemoApp">
    <outer></outer>
</div>

<script type="text/javascript">

    var app = angular.module('DemoApp',[]);

    app.directive('outer',function(){
        return {

            restrict:'E',
            template: '<div><h1>Outer</h1><inner></inner></div>',
        }});

    app.directive('inner',function(){
        return {

            restrict:'E',
            template: '<div><h1>Inner</h1></div>',
```

```
        }
    });
</script>

</body>
</html>
```

Code Explanation:

1. We are creating a directive called "outer" which will behave as our parent directive. This directive will then make a call to the "inner" directive.

2. The restrict:'E' is required by angular to ensure that the data from the inner directive is available to the outer directive. The letter 'E' is the short form of the word 'Element'.

3. Here we are creating the inner directive which displays the text "Inner" in a div tag.

4. In the template for the outer directive (step#4), we are calling the inner directive. So over here we are injecting the template from the inner directive to the outer directive.

5. Finally, we are directly calling out the outer directive.

If the code is executed successfully, the following Output will be shown when you run your code in the browser.

Output:

From the output,

- It can be seen that both the outer and inner directives have been called, and the text in both div tags are displayed.

Handling events in a directive

Events such mouse clicks or button clicks can be handled from within directives itself. This is done using the link function. The link function is what allows the directive to attach itself to the DOM elements in an HTML page.

Syntax:

The syntax of the link element is as shown below

ng-repeat

```
link: function ($scope, element, attrs)
```

The link function normally accepts 3 parameters including the scope, the element that the directive is associated with, and the attributes of the target element.

Let's look at an example of how we can accomplish this.

```html
<!DOCTYPE html>
<html>
<head>
    <meta chrset="UTF 8">
    <title>Event Registration</title>
</head>
<body>

<script src="https://code.angularjs.org/1.6.9/angular-route.js">
</script>
<script src="https://code.angularjs.org/1.6.9/angular.js">
</script>
<script src="https://code.angularjs.org/1.6.9/angular.min.js">
</script>
<script src="https://code.jquery.com/jquery-3.3.1.min.js">
</script>

<h1> Guru99 Global Event</h1>

<div ng-app="DemoApp">
    <div ng-guru="">Click Me</div>
</div>

<script type="text/javascript">

    var app = angular.module('DemoApp',[]);

    app.directive('ngGuru',function(){
        return {

            link:function($scope,element,attrs) {
                element.bind('click',function () {
```

```
                    element.html('You clicked me');
            });}
        }});
</script>

</body>
</html>
```

Code Explanation:

1. We are using the link function as defined in angular to give the ability of the directives to access events in the HTML DOM.

2. We are using the 'element' keyword because we want to respond to an event for an HTML DOM element, which is in our case will be the "div" element. We are then using the "bind" function and saying that we want to add custom functionality to the click event of the element. The 'click' word is the keyword, which is used to denote the click event of any HTML control. For example, the HTML button control has the click event. Since, in our example, we want to add a custom code to the click event of our "dev" tag, we use the 'click' keyword.

3. Here we are saying that we want to substitute the inner HTML of the element (in our case the div element) with the text 'You clicked me!'.

4. Here we are defining our div tag to use the ng-guru custom directive.

If the code is executed successfully, the following Output will be shown when you run your code in the browser.

Output:

- Initially the text 'Click Me' will be shown to the user because this is what has been initially defined in the div tag. When you actually click on the div tag, the below output will be shown

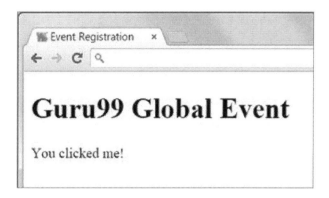

Summary

- One can also create a custom directive which can be used to inject code in the main angular application.
- Custom directives can be made to call members defined in the scope object in a certain controller by using the 'Controller', 'controllerAs' and 'template' keywords.
- Directives can also be nested to provide embedded functionality which may be required depending on the need of the application.
- Directives can also be made re-usable so that they can be used to inject common code that could be required across various web applications.
- Directives can also be used to create custom HTML tags which would have their own functionality defined as per the business requirement.
- Events can also be handled from within directives to handle DOM events such as button and mouse clicks.

Chapter 13: Module

What is an AngularJS Module?

A module defines the application functionality that is applied to the entire HTML page using the ng-app directive. It defines functionality, such as services, directives, and filters, in a way that makes it easy to reuse it in different applications.

In all of our earlier tutorials, you would have noticed the ng-app directive used to define your main Angular application. This is one of the key concepts of modules in Angular.JS.

How to Create a module in AngularJS

Before we start off with what is a module, let's look at an example of an AngularJS application without a module and then understand the need of having modules in your application.

Let's consider creating a file called "DemoController.js" and adding the below code to the file

```
Function Democontroller($scope) {
                          $scope.a=1;
                          $scope.b=2;
                          $scope.c=$scope.b + $scope.a;
             });
```

In the above code, we have created a function called "DemoController" which is going to act as a controller within our application.

In this controller, we are just performing the addition of 2 variables a and b and assigning the addition of these variables to a new variable, c, and assigning it back to the scope object.

Now let's create our main Sample.html, which will be our main application. Let's insert the below code snippet in our HTML page.

```
<body ng-app="">
      <div ng-controller="DemoController">
      <h3> Guru99 Global Event</h3>
      {{c}}
```

In the code above, we are including our DemoController and then invoking the value of the $scope.c variable via an expression.

But notice our ng-app directive, it has a blank value.

- This basically means that all controllers which are called within the context of the ng-app directive can be accessed globally. There is no boundary which separates multiple controllers from each other.
- Now in modern day programming, this is a bad practice to have controllers not attached to any modules and making them globally accessible. There has to be some logical boundary defined for controllers.

And this is where modules come in. Modules are used to create that separation of boundaries and assist in separating controllers based on functionality.

Let's change the code above to implement modules and attach our controller to this module

```
var sampleApp = angular.module('sampleApp',[]);
sampleApp.controller('DemoController', function($scope) {
                              $scope.a=1;
                              $scope.b=2;
                              $scope.c=$scope.b + $scope.a;
                  });
```

Let's note the key differences in the code written above

1. ```
   var sampleApp = angular.module('sampleApp',[]);
   ```

   We are specifically creating an AngularJS module called
   ```

'sampleApp'. This will form a logical boundary for the functionality that this module will contain. So in our above example, we have a module which contains a controller that performs the role of the addition of 2 scope objects. Hence, we can have one module with a logical boundary which says that this module will only perform the functionality of mathematical calculations for the application.

2.
```
sampleApp.controller('DemoController', function($scope)
```

We are now attaching the controller to our AngularJS module "SampleApp". This means that if we don't reference the module 'sampleApp' in our main HTML code, we will not be able to reference the functionality of our controller.

Our main HTML code will not look as shown below

```
<body ng-app="'sampleApp'">
                    <div ng-controller="DemoController">
                    <h3> Guru99 Global Event</h3>
                            {{c}}
```

Let's note the key differences in the code written above and our previous code

```
<body ng-app="'sampleApp'">
```

In our body tag,

- Instead of having an empty ng-app directive, we are now calling the module sampleApp.
- By calling this application module, we can now access the controller 'DemoController' and the functionality present in the demo controller.

Modules and Controllers

In Angular.JS, the pattern used for developing modern day web applications is of creating multiple modules and controllers to logically separate multiple levels of functionality.

Normally modules will be stored in separate Javascript files, which would be different from the main application file.

Let's look at an example of how this can be achieved.

In the example below,

- We will create a file called Utilities.html which will hold 2 modules, one for performing the functionality of addition and the other for performing the functionality of subtraction.
- We are then going to create 2 separate application files and access the Utility file from each application file.
- In one application file we will access the module for addition and in the other, we will access the module for subtraction.

Step 1) Define the code for the multiple modules and controllers.

```
var AdditionApp = angular.module('AdditionApp',[]);
AdditionApp.controller('DemoAddController', function($scope) {
        $scope.a=5;
        $scope.b=6;
        $scope.c=$scope.a + $scope.b;
});
var SubractionApp = angular.module('SubtractionApp',[]);
SubractionApp.controller('DemoSubtractController',
function($scope) {
        $scope.a=8;
        $scope.b=6;
        $scope.d=$scope.a - $scope.b;
});
```

Let's note the key points in the code written above

1.
```
var AdditionApp = angular.module('AdditionApp',[]);
var SubractionApp = angular.module('SubtractionApp',[]);
```

There is 2 separate Angular Module created, one which is given the name 'AdditionApp' and the second one is given the name 'SubtractionApp'.

2.
```
AdditionApp.controller('DemoAddController', function($scope)
SubractionApp.controller('DemoSubtractController',
function($scope)
```

There are 2 separate controllers defined for each module, one is called the DemoAddController and the other is the DemoSubtractController. Each controller has separate logic for addition and subtraction of numbers.

Step 2) Create your main application files. Let's create a file called ApplicationAddition.html and add the below code

```
<!DOCTYPE html>
<html>
<head>
    <meta charset="UTF-8">
    <title>Addition</title>
    <script
src="http://ajax.googleapis.com/ajax/libs/angularjs/1.4.8/angular
.min.js"></script>
    <script src="lib/utilities.js"></script>
</head>
<body>
<div ng-app = "AdditionApp" ng-controller="DemoAddController">
    Addition :{{c}}
<script>
    var AdditionApp = angular.module('AdditionApp',[]);
    AdditionApp.controller('DemoAddController', function($scope)
{
    $scope.a=5;
    $scope.b=6;
    $scope.c=$scope.a + $scope.b;
    });

</script>
</div>
</body>
</html>
```

Let's note the key points in the code written above

1.
```
<script src="/lib/Utilities.js"></script>
```

We are referencing our Utilities.js file in our main application file.

This allows us to reference any AngularJS modules defined in this file.

2.
```
<div ng-app = "AdditionApp" ng-
controller="DemoAddController">
```

We are accessing the 'AdditionApp' module and DemoAddController by using the ng-app directive and the ng-controller respectively.

3.
```
{{c}}
```

Since we are referencing the above-mentioned module and controller we are able to reference the $scope.c variable via an expression. The expression will be the result of the addition of the 2 scope variables a and b which was carried out in the 'DemoAddController' Controller

The same way we will do for subtraction function.

Step 3) Create your main application files. Let's create a file called "ApplicationSubtraction.html" and add the below code

```
<!DOCTYPE html>
<html>
<head>
    <meta charset="UTF-8">
    <title>Addition</title>
    <script
src="http://ajax.googleapis.com/ajax/libs/angularjs/1.4.8/angular
.min.js"></script>
    <script src="lib/utilities.js"></script>
</head>
<body>
<div ng-app = "SubtractionApp" ng-
controller="DemoSubtractController">
    Subtraction :{{d}}
    <script>
        var SubractionApp = angular.module('SubtractionApp',[]);
        SubractionApp.controller('DemoSubtractController',
function($scope) {
            $scope.a=8;
            $scope.b=6;
```

```
            $scope.d=$scope.a - $scope.b;
        });

    </script>
</div>
</body>
</html>
```

Let's note the key points in the code written above

1. ```
<script src="/lib/Utilities.js"></script>
```

   We are referencing our Utilities.js file in our main application file. This allows us to reference any modules defined in this file.

2. ```
<div ng-app = " SubtractionApp " ng-controller="
DemoSubtractController ">
```

   We are accessing the 'SubtractionApp module and DemoSubtractController by using the ng-app directive and the ng-controller respectively.

3. ```
{{d}}
```

   Since we are referencing the above-mentioned module and controller we are able to reference the $scope.d variable via an expression. The expression will be the result of the subtraction of the 2 scope variables a and b which was carried out in the 'DemoSubtractController' Controller

## Summary

- Without the use of AngularJS modules, controllers start having a global scope which leads to bad programming practices.
- Modules are used to separate business logic. Multiple modules can be created to have logically separated within these different modules.
- Each AngularJS module can have its own set of controllers defined and assigned to it.
- When defining modules and controllers, they are normally defined
```

in separate JavaScript files. These JavaScript files are then referenced in the main application file.

Chapter 14: Events

When creating web-based applications, sooner or later your application will need to handle DOM events like mouse clicks, moves, keyboard presses, change events, etc.

AngularJS can add functionality which can be used to handle such events.

For example, if there is a button on the page and you want to process something when the button is clicked, we can use the ng-click event directive.

We will look into Event directives in detail during this course.

The ng-click directive

The "ng-click directive" is used to apply custom behavior to when an element in HTML clicked. This is normally used for buttons because that is the most common place for adding events which respond to clicks performed by the user.

Let's look a simple example of how we can implement the click event.

In this example, we will have a counter variable which will increment in value when the user clicks a button.

```
<!DOCTYPE html>
```

```
<html>
<head>
    <meta chrset="UTF 8">
    <title>Event Registration</title>
</head>
<body ng-app="">

<script src="https://code.angularjs.org/1.6.9/angular.js">
</script>
<script src="https://code.jquery.com/jquery-3.3.1.min.js">
</script>

<h1> Guru99 Global Event</h1>

<button ng-click="count = count + 1" ng-init="count=0">
    Increment
</button>

<div>The Current Count is {{count}}</div>

</body>
</html>
```

Code Explanation:

1. We are first using the ng-init directive to set the value of a local variable count to 0.
2. We are then introducing the ng-click event directive to the button. In this directive, we are writing code to increment the value of the count variable by 1.
3. Here we are displaying the value of the count variable to the user.

If the code is executed successfully, the following Output will be shown when you run your code in the browser.

Output:

From the above output,

- We can see that the button "Increment" is displayed and the value of the count variable is initially zero.
- When you click on the Increment button, the value of the count is incremented accordingly as shown in the output image below.

Showing HTML Elements using ng-show

The ngShow directive is used to show or hide a given HTML element based on the expression provided to the ngShow attribute.

In the background, the element is shown or hidden by removing or adding the .ng-hide CSS class onto the element.

Let's look at an example of how we can use the "ngshow event" directive to display a hidden element.

Setting the ng-show attribute

Setting the isvisible variable

When the function ShowHide is called the isVisible parameter is set to true

Setting the ng-click event

```html
<!DOCTYPE html>
<html>
<head>
    <meta chrset="UTF 8">
    <title>Event Registration</title>
</head>
<body>
<script src="https://code.angularjs.org/1.6.9/angular.js">
</script>
<script src="https://code.jquery.com/jquery-3.3.1.min.js">
</script>

<h1> Guru99 Global Event</h1>
<div ng-app="DemoApp" ng-controller="DemoController">
    <input type="button" value="Show Angular" ng-
click="ShowHide()"/>

    <br><br><div ng-show = "IsVisible">Angular</div>
</div>

<script type="text/javascript">

    var app = angular.module('DemoApp',[]);

    app.controller('DemoController',function($scope){
        $scope.IsVisible = false;

        $scope.ShowHide = function(){
            $scope.IsVisible = $scope.IsVisible = true;
        }
        });
</script>

</body>
</html>
```

Code Explanation:

1. We are attaching the ng-click event directive to the button element. Over here we are referencing a function called "ShowHide" which is defined in our controller – DemoController.

2. We are attaching the ng-show attribute to a div tag which contains the text Angular. This is the tag which we are going to show/hide based on the ng-show attribute.

3. In the controller, we are attaching the "IsVisible" member variable to the scope object. This attribute will be passed to the ng-show angular attribute (step#2) to control the visibility of the div control. We are initially setting this to false so that when the page is first displayed the div tag will be hidden.

   Note:- When the attributes ng-show is set to true, the subsequent control which in our case is the div tag will be shown to the user. When the ng-show attribute is set to false the control will be hidden from the user.

4. We are adding code to the ShowHide function which will set the IsVisible member variable to true so that the div tag can be shown to the user.

If the code is executed successfully, the following Output will be shown when you run your code in the browser.

Output:1

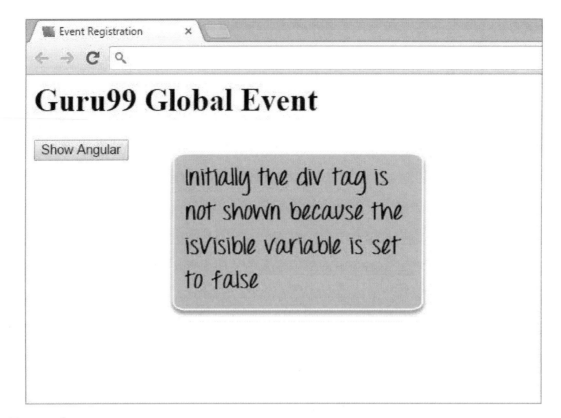

From the output,

- You can initially see that the div tag which has the text "AngularJS" is not shown and this is because the isVisible scope object is initially set to false which is then subsequently passed to the ng-show directive of the div tag.
- When you click on the "Show AngularJS" button, it changes the isVisible member variable to become true and hence the text "Angular" becomes visible to the user. The below output will be shown to the user.

The output now shows the div tag with the Angular text.

Hiding HTML Elements using ng-hide

Just like the ngShow directive, there is also the ng-hide directive. With ng-show the element is shown if the expression is true, it will hide if it is false.

On the other hand with ng-hide, the element is hidden if the expression is true and it will be shown if it is false.

Let's look at the similar example as the one shown for ngShow to showcase how the ngHide attribute can be used.

Setting the ng-show attribute

Setting the isvisible variable

When the function ShowHide is called the isVisible parameter is set to true

Setting the ng-click event

```html
<!DOCTYPE html>
<html>
<head>
    <meta chrset="UTF 8">
    <title>Event Registration</title>
</head>
<body>
<script src="https://code.angularjs.org/1.6.9/angular.js">
</script>
<script src="https://code.jquery.com/jquery-3.3.1.min.js">
</script>

<h1> Guru99 Global Event</h1>
<div ng-app="DemoApp" ng-controller="DemoController">
    <input type="button" value="Hide Angular" ng-click="ShowHide()"/>

    <br><br><div ng-hide="IsVisible">Angular</div>
</div>

<script type="text/javascript">

    var app = angular.module('DemoApp',[]);

    app.controller('DemoController',function($scope){
        $scope.IsVisible = false;

        $scope.ShowHide = function(){
            $scope.IsVisible = $scope.IsVisible = true;
        }
        });
</script>

</body>
</html>
```

Code Explanation:

1. We are attaching the ng-click event directive to the button element. Over here we are referencing a function called ShowHide which is defined in our controller – DemoController.

2. We are attaching the ng-hide attribute to a div tag which contains the text Angular. This is the tag, which we are going to show/hide based on the ng-show attribute.

3. In the controller, we are attaching the isVisible member variable to the scope object. This attribute will be passed to the ng-show angular attribute to control the visibility of the div control. We are initially setting this to false so that when the page is first displayed the div tag will be hidden.

4. We are adding code to the ShowHide function which will set the IsVisible member variable to true so that the div tag can be shown to the user.

If the code is executed successfully, the following Output will be shown when you run your code in the browser.

Output:

From the output,

- You can initially see that the div tag which has the text "AngularJs" is initially shown because the property value of false is sent to the ng-hide directive.
- When we click on the "Hide Angular" button the property value of true will sent to the ng-hide directive. Hence the below output will be shown, in which the word "Angular" will be hidden.

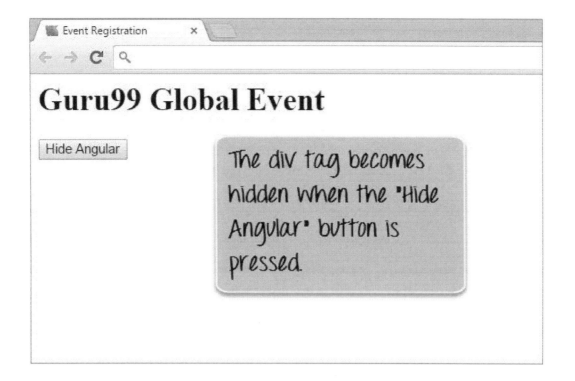

AngularJS Event Listener Directives

You can add AngularJS event listeners to your HTML elements by using one or more of these directives:

- ng-blur
- ng-change
- ng-click
- ng-copy
- ng-cut
- ng-dblclick
- ng-focus
- ng-keydown
- ng-keypress
- ng-keyup
- ng-mousedown
- ng-mouseenter
- ng-mouseleave
- ng-mousemove

- ng-mouseover
- ng-mouseup
- ng-paste

Summary

- Events directives are used in Angular to add custom code to respond to events generated by user intervention such as button clicks, keyboard and mouse clicks, etc.
- The most common event directive is the ng-click directive which is used to handle click events. The most common use of this is for button clicks wherein code can be added to respond to a button click.
- HTML elements can also be hidden or shown to the user accordingly by using the ng-show and ng-hide angular attributes.

Chapter 15: Routing with Parameters

Before we start with routing, let's just have a quick overview on Single-Page Applications.

What is Single Page Applications?

Single page applications or (SPAs) are web applications that load a single HTML page and dynamically update the page based on the user interaction with the web application.

What is Routing in AngularJS?

In AngularJS, routing is what allows you to create Single Page Applications.

- AngularJS routes enable you to create different URLs for different content in your application.
- AngularJS routes allow one to show multiple contents depending on which route is chosen.
- A route is specified in the URL after the # sign.

Let's take an example of a site which is hosted via the URL **http://example.com/index.html**.

On this page, you would host the main page of your application. Suppose if the application was organizing an Event and one wanted to see what the various events on display are, or wanted to see the details of a particular event or delete an event. In a Single Page application, when routing is enabled, all of this functionality would be available via the following links

http://example.com/index.html#ShowEvent

http://example.com/index.html#DisplayEvent

http://example.com/index.html#DeleteEvent

The # symbol would be used along with the different routes (ShowEvent, DisplayEvent, and DeleteEvent).

- So if the user wanted to see all Events, they would be directed to the link (**http://example.com/index.html#ShowEvent**), else
- If they wanted to just see a particular event they would be re-directed to the link (
  http://example.com/index.html#DisplayEvent) or
- If they wanted to delete an event, they would be directed to the link **http://example.com/index.html#DeleteEvent**.

Note that the main URL stays the same.

Adding Angular Route ($routeProvider)

So as we discussed earlier, routes in AngularJS are used to route the user to a different view of your application. And this routing is done on the same HTML page so that the user has the experience that he has not left the page.

In order to implement routing the following main steps have to be implemented in your application in any specific order.

1. Reference to angular-route.js. This is a JavaScript file developed by Google that has all the functionality of routing. This needs to be placed in your application so that it can reference all of the main modules which are required for routing.

2. The next important step is to add a dependency to the ngRoute

module from within your application. This dependency is required so that routing functionality can be used within the application. If this dependency is not added, then one will not be able to use routing within the angular.JS application.

Below is the general syntax of this statement. This is just a normal declaration of a module with the inclusion of the ngRoute keyword.

```
var module = angular.module("sampleApp", ['ngRoute']);
```

3. The next step would be to configure your $routeProvider. This is required for providing the various routes in your application.

   Below is the general syntax of this statement which is very self-explanatory. It just states that when the relevant path is chosen, use the route to display the given view to the user.

```
when(path, route)
```

4. Links to your route from within your HTML page. In your HTML page, you will add reference links to the various available routes in your application.

```
<a href="#/route1">Route 1</a><br/>
```

5. Finally would be the inclusion of the ng-view directive, which would normally be in a div tag. This would be used to inject the content of the view when the relevant route is chosen.

Now, let's look at an example of routing using the above-mentioned steps.

In our example,

We will present 2 links to the user,

- One is to display the topics for an **Angular JS** course, and the other is for the **Node.js** course.
- When the user clicks either link, the topics for that course will be

displayed.

Step 1) Include the angular-route file as a script reference.

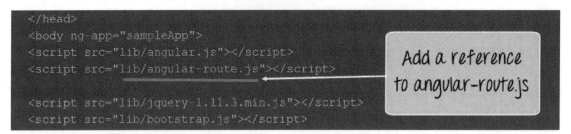

This route file is necessary in order to make use of the functionalities of having multiple routes and views. This file can be downloaded from the angular.JS website.

Step 2) Add href tags which will represent links to "Angular JS Topics" and "Node JS Topics."

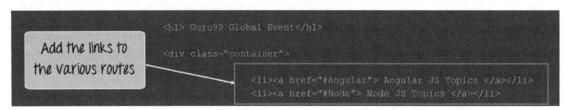

Step3) Add a div tag with the ng-view directive which will represent the view.

This will allow the corresponding view to be injected whenever the user clicks on either the "Angular JS Topics" or "Node JS Topics."

Step 4) In your script tag for AngularJS, add the "ngRoute module" and the "$routeProvider" service.

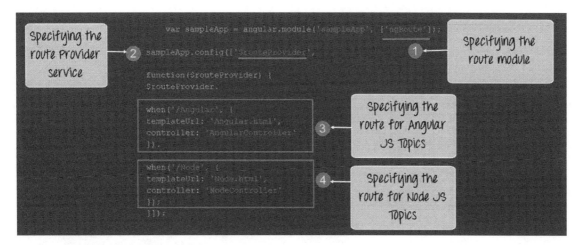

Code Explanation:

1. The first step is to ensure to include the "ngRoute module." With this in place, Angular will automatically handle the routing in your application. The ngRoute module which is developed by Google has all of the functionality which allows for routing to be possible. By adding this module, the application will automatically understand all of the routing commands.

2. The $routeprovider is a service that angular uses to listen in the background to the routes which are called. So when the user clicks a link, the routeprovider will detect this and then decide on which route to take.

3. Create one route for the Angular link – This block means that when the Angular link is clicked, inject the file Angular.html and also use the Controller 'AngularController' to process any business logic.

4. Create one route for the Node link – This block means that when the Node link is clicked, inject the file Node.html and also use the Controller 'NodeController' to process any business logic.

Step 5) Next is to add controllers to process the business logic for both the AngularController and NodeController.

In each controller, we are creating an array of key-values pairs to store the Topic names and descriptions for each course. The array variable 'tutorial' is added to the scope object for each controller.

Creating the list of Angular JS topics — 1

Creating the list of Node JS topics — 2

```html
<!DOCTYPE html>
<html>
<head>
    <meta chrset="UTF 8">
</head>
<body ng-app="sampleApp">
<title>Event Registration</title>
<script src="https://code.angularjs.org/1.6.9/angular-route.js">
</script>
<script src="https://code.angularjs.org/1.6.9/angular.min.js">
</script>
<script src="https://code.angularjs.org/1.6.9/angular.js">
</script>

<h1> Guru99 Global Event</h1>

<div class="container">
    <ul>
        <li><a href="#Angular">Angular JS Topics</a></li>
        <li><a href="#Node.html">Node JS Topics</a></li>
    </ul>
    <div ng-view></div>
</div>

<script>
    var sampleApp = angular.module('sampleApp',['ngRoute']);
    sampleApp.config(['$routeProvider',

        function($routeProvider){
        $routeProvider.
        when('/Angular',{
            templateUrl : '/Angular.html',
            controller: 'AngularController'
```

```
        }).
        when("/Node", {
            templateUrl: '/Node.html',
            controller: 'NodeController'
        });
    }]);
    sampleApp.controller('AngularController',function($scope) {

        $scope.tutorial = [
            {Name:"Controllers",Description :"Controllers in
action"},
            {Name:"Models",Description :"Models and binding
data"},
            {Name:"Directives",Description :"Flexibility of
Directives"}
        ]
    });


    sampleApp.controller('NodeController',function($scope){

        $scope.tutorial = [
            {Name:"Promises",Description :"Power of Promises"},
            {Name:"Event",Description :"Event of Node.js"},
            {Name:"Modules",Description :"Modules in Node.js"}
            ]
    });

</script>
</body>
</html>
```

Step 6) Create pages called Angular.html and Node.html. For each page we are carrying out the below steps.

These steps will ensure that all of the key-value pairs of the array are displayed on each page.

1. Using the ng-repeat directive to go through each key-value pair defined in the tutorial variable.
2. Displaying the name and description of each key-value pair.

- **Angular.html**

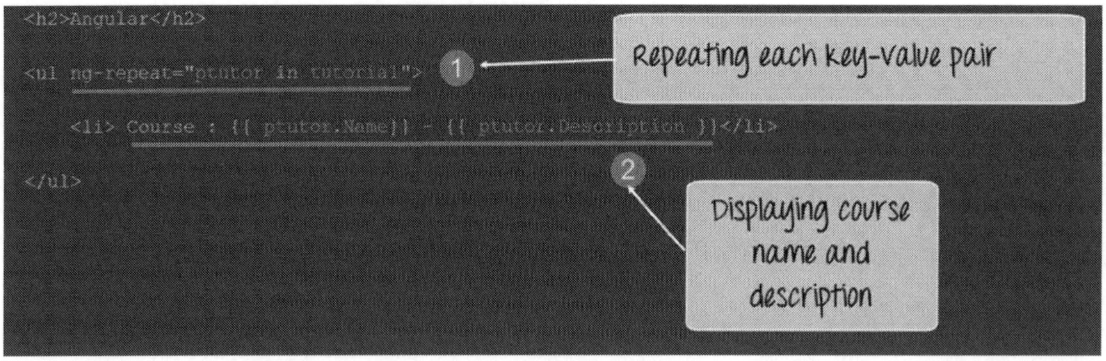

Repeating each key-value pair

Displaying course name and description

```
</h2>Anguler</h2>
<ul ng-repeat="ptutor in tutorial">
      <li>Course : {{ptutor.Name}} - {{ptutor.Description}}</li>
</ul>
```

- **Node.html**

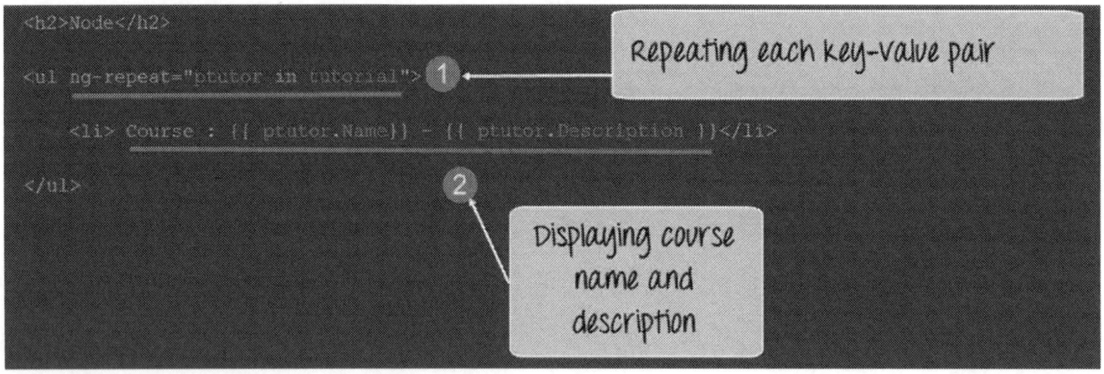

Repeating each key-value pair

Displaying course name and description

```
<h2>Node</h2>
<ul ng-repeat="ptutor in tutorial">
      <li>Course : {{ptutor.Name}} - {{ptutor.Description}}</li>
</ul>
```

If the code is executed successfully, the following Output will be shown when you run your code in the browser.

Output:

If you click on the AngularJS Topics link the below output will be displayed.

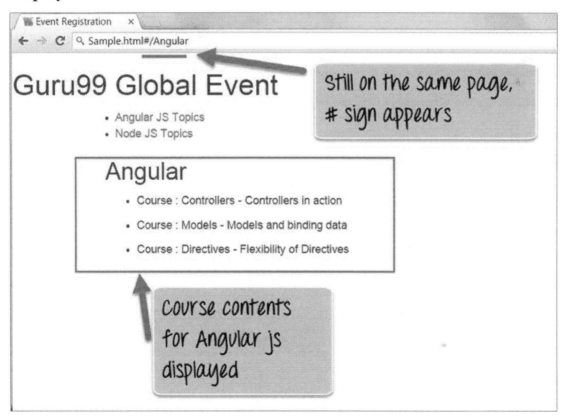

The output clearly shows that,

- When the "Angular JS Topics" link is clicked, the routeProvider that we declared in our code decides that the Angular.html code should be injected.
- This code will be injected into the "div" tag, which contains the ng-view directive. Also, the content for the course description comes from the "tutorial variable" which was part of the scope object defined in the AngularController.
- When one clicks on the Node.js Topics, the same result will take place, and the view for Node.js topics will be manifested.
- Also, notice that the page URL stays the same, it's only the route after the # tag which changes. And this is the concept of single page applications. The #hash tag in the URL is a separator which separates the route (which in our case is 'Angular' as shown in above image) and main HTML page(Sample.html)

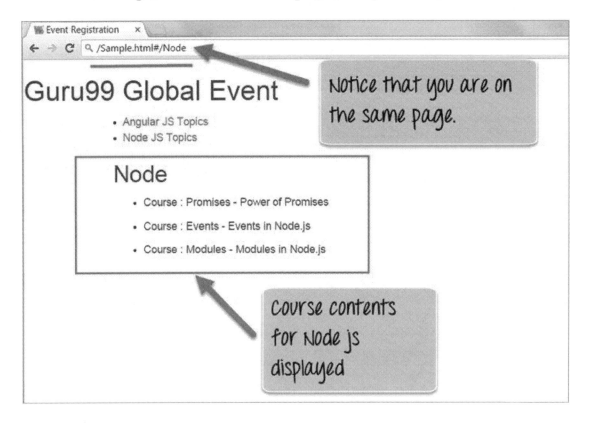

Creating a default route

Routing in AngularJS also provides the facility to have a default route.

This is the route which is chosen if there is no match for the existing route.

The default route is created by adding the following condition when defining the $routeProvider service.

The below syntax just simply means to redirect to a different page if any of the existing routes don't match.

```
otherwise ({
    redirectTo: 'page'
});
```

Let's use the same example above and add a default route to our $routeProvider service.

```
function($routeProvider) {
$routeProvider.

when('/Angular', {
templateUrl: 'Angular.html',
controller: 'AngularController'
}).

when('/Node', {
templateUrl: 'Node.html',
controller: 'NodeController'
}).
otherwise({
    redirectTo: '/Angular'
});

}]);
```

Make the angular section the default view shown

```
function($routeProvider){
$routeProvider.

when('/Angular',{
templateUrl : 'Angular.html',
controller: 'AngularController'
}).

when("/Node", {
templateUrl: 'Node.html',
```

```
controller: 'NodeController'
}).
otherwise({
    redirectTo:'/Angular'
});
}]);
```

Code Explanation:

1. Here we are using the same code as above with the only difference
   is that we are using the otherwise statement and the "redirectTo"
   option to specify which view should be loaded if no route is
   specified. In our case we want the '/Angular' view to be shown.

If the code is executed successfully, the following Output will be shown
when you run your code in the browser.

Output:

From the output,

- You can clearly see that the default view shown is the angular JS view.
- This is because when the page loads it goes to the 'otherwise' option in the $routeProvider function and loads the '/Angular' view.

Accessing parameters from the route

Angular also provides the functionality to provide parameters during routing. The parameters are added to the end of the route in the URL, for example, **http://guru99/index.html#/Angular/1**. In this example

1. **, http://guru99/index.html** is our main application URL
2. The # symbol is the separator between the main application URL and the route.
3. Angular is our route
4. And finally '1' is the parameter which is added to our route

The syntax of how parameters look in the URL is shown below:

HTMLPage#/route/parameter

Here you will notice that the parameter is passed after the route in the URL.

So in our example, above for the Angular JS topics, we can pass a parameter's as shown below

Sample.html#/Angular/1

Sample.html#/Angular/2

Sample.html#/Angular/3

Here the parameters of 1, 2 and 3 can actually represent the topicid.

Let's look in detail at how we can implement this.

Step 1) Add the following code to your view

1. Add a table to show all the topics for the Angular JS course to the user

2. Add a table row for showing the topic "Controllers." For this row, change the href tag to "Angular/1" which means that when the user clicks this topic, the parameter 1 will be passed in the URL along with the route.

3. Add a table row for showing the topic "Models." For this row, change the href tag to "Angular/2" which means that when the user clicks this topic, the parameter 2 will be passed in the URL

along with the route.

4. Add a table row for showing the topic "Directives." For this row, change the href tag to "Angular/3" which means that when the user clicks this topic, the parameter 3 will be passed in the URL along with the route.

Step 2) In the routeprovider service function add the:topicId to denote that any parameter passed in the URL after the route should be assigned to the variable topicId.

```
var sampleApp = angular.module('sampleApp', ['ngRoute']);

sampleApp.config(['$routeProvider',

function ($routeProvider) {
    $routeProvider.
    when('/Angular/:topicId', {

        templateUrl: 'Angular.html',
        controller: 'AngularController'
    })
}]);
```

Make sure to enter a parameter to the URL

Step 3) Add the necessary code to the controller

1. Make sure to first add the "$routeParams" as a parameter when defining the controller function. This parameter will have access

to all of the route parameters passed in the URL.

2. The "routeParams" parameter has a reference to the topicId object, which is passed as a route parameter. Here we are attaching the '$routeParams.topicId' variable to our scope object as the variable '$scope.tutotialid'. This is being done so that it can be referenced in our view via the tutorialid variable.

```html
<!DOCTYPE html>
<html>
<head>

    <meta chrset="UTF 8">
    <title>Event Registration</title>
</head>
<body ng-app="sampleApp">

<script src="https://code.angularjs.org/1.6.9/angular-route.js">
</script>
<script src="https://code.angularjs.org/1.6.9/angular.min.js">
</script>
<script src="lib/bootstrap.js"></script>
<script src="lib/bootstrap.css"></script>

<h1> Guru99 Global Event</h1>
<table class="table table-striped">
    <thead>
    <tr> <th>#</th><th>Angular JS topic</th><th>Description</th>
<th></th> </tr> </thead>
    <tbody>
    <tr>
        <td>1</td><td>1</td><td>Controllers</td>
        <td><a href="#Angular/1">Topic details</a></td>
    </tr>
    <tr>
        <td>2</td><td>2</td><td>Models</td>
        <td><a href="#Angular/2">Topic details</a></td>
    </tr>
    <tr>
```

```
        <td>3</td><td>3</td><td>Directives</td>
        <td><a href="#Angular/3">Topic details</a></td>
    </tr>
    </tbody>
</table>

<script>
    var sampleApp = angular.module('sampleApp',['ngRoute']);

    sampleApp.config(
        function($routeProvider){
            $routeProvider.
            when('/Angular/:topicId',{
                templateUrl : 'Angular.html',
                controller: 'AngularController'
            })
        });


sampleApp.controller('AngularController',function($scope,$routePa
rams) {

        $scope.tutorialid=$routeParams.topicId

    });
</script>
</body>
</html>
```

Step 4) Add the expression to display the tutorialid variable in the Angular.html page.

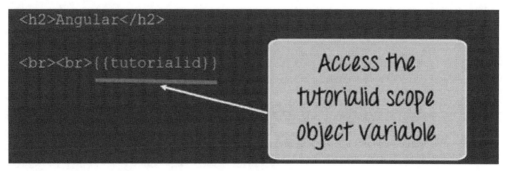

```
<h2>Anguler</h2>
<br><br>{{tutorialid}}
```

If the code is executed successfully, the following Output will be shown when you run your code in the browser.

Output:

In the output screen,

- If you click on the Topic Details link for the first topic, the number 1 gets appended to the URL.
- This number will be then taken as a "routeparam" argument by the Angular.JS routeprovider service and can then be accessed by our controller.

Using Angular $route service

The $route service allows you to access the properties of the route. The $route service is available as a parameter when the function is defined in the controller. The general syntax of how the $route parameter is available from the controller is shown below;

```
myApp.controller('MyController',function($scope,$route)
```

1. myApp is the angular.JS module defined for your applications
2. MyController is the name of the controller defined for your

application

3. Just like the $scope variable is made available for your application, which is used to pass information from the controller to the view. The $route parameter is used to access the properties of the route.

Let's have a look on how we can use the $route service.

In this example,

- We are going to create a simple custom variable called "mytext," which will contain the string "This is angular."
- We are going to attach this variable to our route. And later we are going to access this string from our controller using the $route service and then subsequently use the scope object to display that in our view.

So, let's see the steps which we need to carry out to achieve this.

Step 1) Add a custom key-value pair to the route. Here, we are adding a key called 'mytext' and assigning it a value of "This is angular."

```
sampleApp.config(['$routeProvider',

function($routeProvider) {
    $routeProvider.
    when('/Angular/:topicId', {
        mytext:"This is angular",

        templateUrl: 'Angular.html',
        controller: 'AngularController'
    })
}]);
```

Create a key-value pair in the routeProvider function

Step 2) Add the relevant code to the controller

1. Add the $route parameter to the controller function. The $route parameter is a key parameter defined in angular, which allows one to access the properties of the route.
2. The "mytext" variable which was defined in the route can be

accessed via the $route.current reference. This is then assigned to the 'text' variable of the scope object. The text variable can then be accessed from the view accordingly.

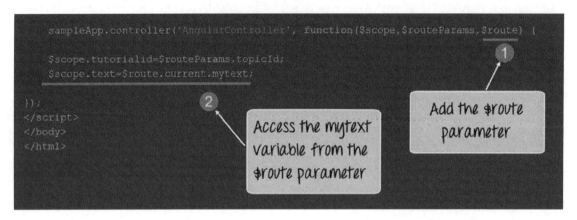

```
sampleApp.controller('AngularController', function($scope,$routeParams,$route) {

    $scope.tutorialid=$routeParams.topicId;
    $scope.text=$route.current.mytext;              ①

});                                            ②
</script>
</body>
</html>
```

② Access the mytext variable from the $route parameter

① Add the $route parameter

```html
<!DOCTYPE html>
<html>
<head>

    <meta chrset="UTF 8">
    <title>Event Registration</title>
</head>
<body ng-app="sampleApp">

<script src="https://code.angularjs.org/1.6.9/angular-route.js">
</script>
<script src="https://code.angularjs.org/1.6.9/angular.min.js">
</script>
<script src="lib/bootstrap.js"></script>
<script src="lib/bootstrap.css"></script>

<h1> Guru99 Global Event</h1>
<table class="table table-striped">
    <thead>
    <tr> <th>#</th><th>Angular JS topic</th><th>Description</th>
<th></th> </tr> </thead>
    <tbody>
    <tr>
        <td>l</td><td>l</td><td>Controllers</td>
        <td><a href="#Angular/1">Topic details</a></td>
    </tr>
    <tr>
        <td>2</td><td>2</td><td>Models</td>
        <td><a href="#Angular/2">Topic details</a></td>
    </tr>
```

```
    <tr>
        <td>3</td><td>3</td><td>Directives</td>
        <td><a href="#Angular/3">Topic details</a></td>
    </tr>
    </tbody>
</table>

<script>
    var sampleApp = angular.module('sampleApp',['ngRoute']);

    sampleApp.config(['$routeProvider',
        function($routeProvider){
            $routeProvider.
            when('/Angular/:topicId',{
                mytext:"This is angular",
                templateUrl : 'Angular.html',
                controller: 'AngularController'
            })
        }]);



sampleApp.controller('AngularController',function($scope,$routePa
rams,$route) {

        $scope.tutorialid=$routeParams.topicId;
        $scope.text=$route.current.mytext;

    });
</script>
</body>
</html>
```

Step 3) Add a reference to the text variable from the scope object as an expression. This will be added to our Angular.html page as shown below.

This will cause the text "This is angular" to be injected into the view. The {{tutorialid}} expression is the same as that seen in the previous topic and this will display the number '1'.

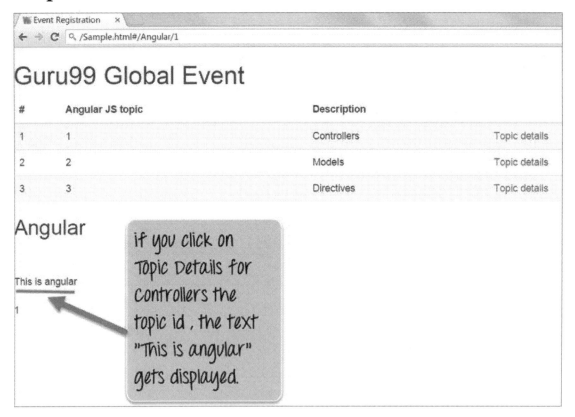

```
<h2>Angular</h2>

<br><br>{{text}}



<br><br>{{tutorialid}}
```

Access the text variable as an expression in your view

```
<h2>Anguler</h2>
<br><br>{{text}}
<br><br>
```

If the code is executed successfully, the following Output will be shown when you run your code in the browser.

Output:

Event Registration ×

← → C ﹒/Sample.html#/Angular/1

Guru99 Global Event

#	Angular JS topic	Description	
1	1	Controllers	Topic details
2	2	Models	Topic details
3	3	Directives	Topic details

Angular

This is angular

1

if you click on Topic Details for Controllers the topic id , the text "This is angular" gets displayed.

From the output,

- We can see that the text "This is angular" also gets displayed when we click on any of the links in the table. The topic id also gets displayed at the same time as the text.

Enabling HTML5 Routing

HTML5 routing is used basically to create clean URL. It means the removal of the hashtag from the URL. So the routing URLs, when HTML5 routing is used, would appear as shown below

Sample.html/Angular/1

Sample.html/Angular/2

Sample.html/Angular/3

This concept is normally known as presenting pretty URL to the user.

There are 2 main steps which need to be carried out for HTML5 routing.

1. Configuring $locationProvider
2. Setting our base for relative links

Let's look into the detail of how to carry out the above-mentioned steps in our example above

Step 1) Add the relevant code to the angular module

1. Add a baseURL constant to the application – This is required for HTML5 routing so that the application knows what the base location of the application is.
2. Add the $locationProvider services. This service allows you to define the html5Mode.
3. Set the html5Mode of the $locationProvider service to true.

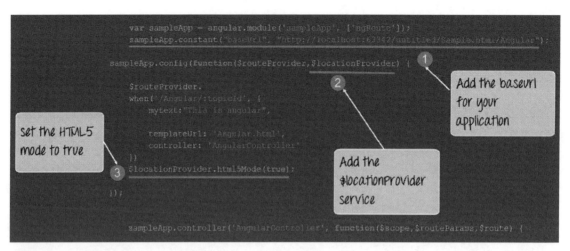

```
var sampleApp = angular.module('sampleApp', ['ngRoute']);
sampleApp.constant("baseUrl", "http://localhost:63942/untitled/Sample.html/Angular");

sampleApp.config(function($routeProvider,$locationProvider) {                    ①

    $routeProvider.
    when('/Angular/:topicId', {                           ②
        mytext:"This is angular",

        templateUrl: 'Angular.html',
        controller: 'AngularController'
    })
    $locationProvider.html5Mode(true);        ③

});

sampleApp.controller('AngularController', function($scope,$routeParams,$route) {
```

Callout 1: Add the baseurl for your application

Callout 2: Add the $locationProvider service

Callout 3 (left): set the HTML5 mode to true

Step 2) Remove all the #tags for the links ('Angular/1', 'Angular/2', 'Angular/3') to create easy to read URL.

```
<table class="table table-striped">
    <thead>
    <tr> <th>#</th><th>Angular JS topic</th><th>Description</th><th></th>
    </tr> </thead>
    <tbody>
    <tr>
        <td>1</td><td>1</td><td>Controllers</td>
        <td><a href="Angular/1">Topic details</a></td>
    </tr>
    <tr>
        <td>2</td><td>2</td><td>Models</td>
        <td><a href="Angular/2">Topic details</a></td>
    </tr>
    <tr>
        <td>3</td><td>3</td><td>Directives</td>
        <td><a href="Angular/3">Topic details</a></td>
    </tr>
    </tbody>
</table>
```

Callout: Remove all #tags from the href links

```html
<!DOCTYPE html>
<html>
<head>

    <meta chrset="UTF 8">
    <title>Event Registration</title>
</head>
<body ng-app="sampleApp">

<script src="https://code.angularjs.org/1.6.9/angular-route.js">
</script>
<script src="https://code.angularjs.org/1.6.9/angular.min.js">
</script>
<script src="lib/bootstrap.js"></script>
<script src="lib/bootstrap.css"></script>
```

```html
<h1> Guru99 Global Event</h1>
<table class="table table-striped">
    <thead>
    <tr> <th>#</th><th>Angular JS topic</th><th>Description</th>
<th></th> </tr> </thead>
    <tbody>
    <tr>
        <td>1</td><td>1</td><td>Controllers</td>
        <td><a href="Angular/1">Topic details</a></td>
    </tr>
    <tr>
        <td>2</td><td>2</td><td>Models</td>
        <td><a href="Angular/2">Topic details</a></td>
    </tr>
    <tr>
        <td>3</td><td>3</td><td>Directives</td>
        <td><a href="Angular/3">Topic details</a></td>
    </tr>
    </tbody>
</table>

<script>
    var sampleApp = angular.module('sampleApp',['ngRoute']);

sampleApp.constant("baseUrl","http://localhost:63342/untitled/Sam
ple.html/Angular");

    sampleApp.config(
        function($routeProvider,$locationProvider){
            $routeProvider.
            when('/Angular/:topicId',{
                templateUrl : 'Angular.html',
                controller: 'AngularController'
            })
        });


sampleApp.controller('AngularController',function($scope,$routePa
rams,$route) {

        $scope.tutorialid=$routeParams.topicId

    });
</script>
</body>
</html>
```

If the code is executed successfully, the following Output will be shown when you run your code in the browser.

Output:

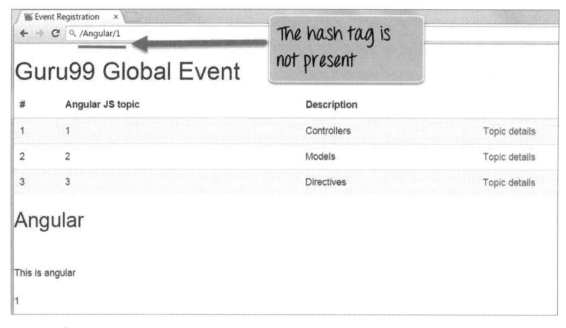

From the output,

- You can see that the # tag is not there when accessing the application.

Summary

- Routing is used to present different views to the user on the same web page. This is basically the concept used in Single page applications which are implemented for almost all modern day web applications
- A default route can be set-up for angular.JS routing. It is used to determine what will be the default view to be shown to the user
- Parameters can be passed to the route via the URL as route parameters. These parameters are then subsequently accessed by using the $routeParams parameter in the controller
- The $route service can be used to define custom key-value pairs in the route which can then be subsequently accessed from within the view

- HTML5 routing is used to remove the #tag from routing URL in angular to form pretty URL

Chapter 16: AJAX Call

AJAX is the short form of Asynchronous JavaScript and XML. AJAX was primarily designed for updating parts of a web page, without reloading the whole page.

The reason for designing this technology was to reduce the number of round trips which were made between the client and the server and the number of entire page refresh which used to take place whenever a user required certain information.

AJAX allowed web pages to be updated asynchronously by exchanging small amounts of data with the server behind the scenes. This meant that it was possible to update parts of a web page, without reloading the whole page.

Many modern-day web applications actually follow this technique for refreshing the page or getting data from the server.

High-level interactions with servers using $resource

Angular provides two different APIs to handle Ajax requests. They are

- $resource
- $http

We will look at the "$resource" property in Angular, which is used to interact with servers at a high level.

When we talk about interacting at a higher level, it means that we will only be bothered about what the server has to offer regarding functionality and not about what exactly the server does in detail with regards to this functionality.

For example, if the server was hosting an application which maintains the employee information of a certain company, the server might expose functionality to clients such as GetEmployeeDetails, SetEmployeeDetails, etc.

So at a high level, we know what these two functions can do, and we can invoke them using the $resource property. But then we don't know exactly the details of the "GetEmployeeDetails" and the "SetEmployeeDetails functions", and how it is implemented.

The above explanation explains what is known as a REST-based architecture.

- REST is known as Representational State Transfer, which is an architecture followed in many modern web-based systems.
- It means that you can use the normal HTTP verbs of GET, POST, PUT and DELETE to work with a web-based application.

So let's assume, we have a web application that maintains a list of Events.

If we wanted to get to the list of all of the events,

- The web application can expose a URL such as **http://example/events** and
- We can use the "GET" verb to get the entire list of events if the application is following a REST based architecture.

So for example, if there was an Event with an ID of 1, then we can get the details of this event via the URL. **http://example/events/1**

What is the $resource object

The $resource object in Angular helps in working with servers that serve applications on a REST based architecture.

The basic syntax of the @resource statement along with the various functions are given below

Syntax of @resource statement

```
var resource Object = $resource(url);
```

Once you have the resourceObject at hand, you can use the below functions to make the required REST calls.

1. get([params], [success], [error]) – This can be used to make the standard GET call.

2. save([params], postData, [success], [error]) - This can be used to make the standard POST call.

3. query([params], [success], [error]) - This can be used to make the standard GET call, but an array is returned as part of the response.

4. remove([params], postData, [success], [error]) - This can be used to make the standard DELETE call.

In all of the functions given below the 'params' parameter can be used to provide the required parameters, which need to be passed in the URL.

For example,

- Suppose you pass a value of Topic: 'Angular' as a 'param' in the get function as
- get('**http://example/events**' ,'{ Topic: 'Angular' }')
- The URL **http://example/events?Topic=Angular** gets invoked as part of the get function.

How to use $resource property

In order to use the $resource property, the following steps need to be followed:

Step 1) The file "angular-resource.js" needs to be downloaded from the Angular.JS site and has to place in the application.

Step 2) The application module should declare a dependency on the "ngResource" module in order to use the $resource.

In the following example, we are calling the "ngResource" module from our 'DemoApp' application.

```
angular.module(DemoApp,['ngResource']); //DemoApp is our main
module
```

Step 3) Calling the $resource() function with your REST endpoint, as shown in the following example.

If you do this, then the $resource object will have the ability to invoke the necessary functionality exposed by the REST endpoints.

The following example calls the endpoint URL:
http://example/events/1

```
angular.module('DemoApp.services').factory('Entry',
function($resource)
{
      return $resource('/example/Event/:1); // Note the full
endpoint address
});
```

In the example above the following things are being done

1. When defining the Angular application, a service is being created by using the statement 'DemoApp.services' where DemoApp is the name given to our Angular application.

2. The .factory method is used to create the details of this new service.

3. 'Entry' is the name we are giving to our service which can be any name you want to provide.

4. In this service, we are creating a function which is going to call the $resource API

5. $resource('/example/Event/:1).

   The $resource function is a service which is used to call a REST endpoint. The REST endpoint is normally a URL. In the above function, we are using the URL (/example /Event/:1) as our REST endpoint. Our REST endpoint(/example /Event/:1) denotes that there is an Event application sitting on our main site "example". This Event application is developed by using a REST-based architecture.

6. The result of the function call is a resource class object. The resource object will now have the functions (get() , query() , save() , remove(), delete()) which can be invoked.

Step 4) We can now use the methods which were returned in the above step(which are the get() , query() , save() , remove(), delete()) in our controller.

In the below code snippet, we are using the get() function as an example

Let's look at the code which can make use of the get() function.

```
angular.module('DemoApp.controllers',[]);
angular.module('DemoApp.controllers').controller('DemoController'
,function($scope, MyFunction) {
  var obj = MyFunction.get({ 1: $scope.id }, function() {
    console.log(obj);
  });
```

In the above step,

- The get() function in the above snippet issues a GET request to / example /Event/:1.
- The parameter:1 in the URL is replaced with $scope.id.
- The function get() will return an empty object which is populated automatically when the actual data comes from the server.
- The second argument to get() is a callback which is executed when the data arrives from the server. The possible output of the entire code would be a JSON object which would return the list of Events exposed from the "example" website.

    An example of what can be returned is shown below

```
{
{ 'EventName' : 'Angular , 'EventDescription' : 'Angular
Basics'},
{ 'EventName' : 'Node , 'EventDescription' : 'Node Basics'},
{ 'EventName' : 'Programming in C++ , 'EventDescription' :
'C++ Basics'}
```

```
}
```

Low-level server interactions with $http

The $http is another Angular JS service which is used to read data from remote servers. The most popular form of data which is read from servers is data in the JSON format.

Let's assume, that we have a PHP page (**http://example/angular/getTopics.PHP**) that returns the following JSON data

```
"Topics": [
  {
    "Name" : "Controllers",
    "Description" : "Controllers in action"
  },
  {
    "Name" : "Models",
    "Description" : "Binding data using Models"
  },
  {
    "Name" : "Directives",
    "Description" : "Using directives in Angular"
  }
]
```

Let's look at the AngularJS code using $http, which can be used to get the above data from the server

```
<script>
var app = angular.module('myApp', []);
app.controller('AngularCtrl', function($scope, $http) {
    $http.get("http://example/angular/getTopics.PHP")
    .then(function(response)
{
$scope.names = response.data.records;});
});
</script>
```

In the above example

1. We are adding the $http service to our Controller function so that we can use the "get" function of the $http service.
2. We are now using the get function from the HTTP service to get the JSON objects from the URL **http://example /angular/getTopics.PHP**
3. Based on the 'response' object, we are creating a callback function which will return the data records and subsequently we are storing them in the $scope object.
4. We can then use the $scope.names variable from the controller and use it in our view to display the JSON objects accordingly.

Fetching data from a server running SQL and MySQL

Angular can also be used to fetch data from a server running MySQL or SQL.

The idea is that if you have a PHP page connecting to a MySQL database or an Asp.Net page connecting to an MS SQL server database, then you need to ensure both the PHP and the ASP.Net page renders the data in JSON format.

Let's assume, we have a PHP site (**http://example /angular/getTopics.PHP**) serving data from either a MySQL or SQL database.

Step 1) The first step is to ensure that the PHP page takes the data from a MySQL database and serves the data in JSON format.

Step 2) Write the similar code shown above to use the $http service to get the JSON data.

Let's look at the AngularJS code using $http which can be used to get the above data from the server

```
<script>
var app = angular.module('myApp', []);
app.controller('AngularCtrl', function($scope, $http) {
```

```
    $http.get("http://example /angular/getTopics.PHP")
    .then(function(response)
{
        $scope.topics = response.data.records;});
});
</script>
```

Step 3) Render the data in your view using the ng-repeat directive.

Below we are using the ng-repeat directive to go through each of the key-value pairs in the JSON objects returned by the "get" method of the $http service.

For each JSON object, we are displaying the key which is "Name" and the value is "Description".

```
<div ng-app="myApp" ng-controller="AngularCtrl">
<table>
  <tr ng-repeat="x in topics">
    <td>{{ x.Name }}</td>
    <td>{{ x.Description }}</td>
  </tr>
</table>
</div>
```

Summary:

- We have had a look at what a RESTFUL architecture is, which is nothing but a functionality exposed by web applications based on the normal HTTP verbs of GET, POST, PUT and DELETE.
- The $resource object is used with Angular to interact with the RESTFUL web applications at a high level which means that we only invoke the functionality exposed by the web application but don't bother of how the functionality is implemented.
- We also looked at the $http service which can be used to get data from a web application. This is possible because the $http service can work with web applications at a more detailed level.
- Because of the power of the $http service, this can be used to get data from a MySQL or MS SQL Server via a PHP application. The data can then be rendered in a table using the ng-repeat directive.

Chapter 17: Table

Tables are one of the common elements used in HTML when working with web pages.

Tables in HTML are designed using the HTML tag

1. <table> tag – This is the main tag used for displaying the table.
2. <tr> - This tag is used for segregating the rows within the table.
3. <td> - This tag is used for displaying the actual table data.
4. <th> - This is used for the table header data.

Using the above available HTML tags along with AngularJS, we can make it easier to populate table data. In short, the ng-repeat directive is used to fill in table data.

We will look at how to achieve this during this chapter. We will also look at how we can use the orderby and uppercase filters along with using the $index attribute to display Angular table indexes.

Populate & Display Data in a Table

As we discussed in the introduction to this chapter, the basis for creating the table structure in an HTML page remains the same.

The structure of the table is still created using the normal HTML tags of <table>,<tr> , <td> and <th>. However, the data is populated by using the ng-repeat directive in AngularJS.

Let's look a simple example of how we can implement Angular tables.

In this example,

We are going to create an Angular table which will have course topics along with their descriptions.

Step 1) We are first going to add a "style" tag to our HTML page so that the table can be displayed as a proper table.

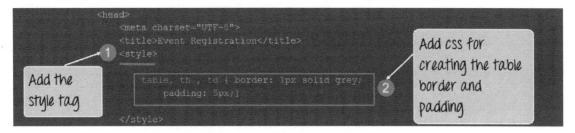

1. The style tag is added to the HTML page. This is the standard way to add any formatting attributes which are required for HTML elements.
2. We are adding two style values to our table.

- One is that there should be a solid border for our Angular table and
- Second is that there should be padding put in place for our Angular table data.

Step 2) The next step is to write the code to generate the table, and it's data.

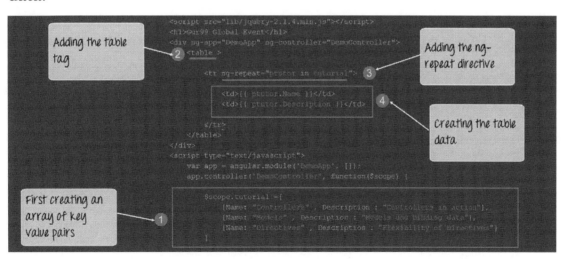

```
<!DOCTYPE html>
<html>
<head>

    <meta chrset="UTF 8">

</head>
<body>
```

```html
<title>Event Registration</title>
<style>
    table,th,td{
        border: 1px solid grey;
        padding:5px;
    }
</style>
<script src="https://code.angularjs.org/1.6.9/angular-route.js">
</script>
<script src="https://code.angularjs.org/1.6.9/angular.min.js">
</script>
<script src="https://code.angularjs.org/1.6.9/angular.js">
</script>
<script src="lib/bootstrap.js"></script>
<script src="lib/bootstrap.css"></script>

<h1> Guru99 Global Event</h1>

<div ng-app="DemoApp" ng-controller="DemoController">
    <table>
        <tr ng-repeat="ptutor in tutorial">
            <td>{{ptutor.Name}}</td>
            <td>{{ptutor.Description}}</td>
        </tr>
    </table>
</div>

<script type="text/javascript">
    var app = angular.module('DemoApp',[]);

    app.controller('DemoController',function($scope) {

        $scope.tutorial = [
            {Name:"Controllers",Description :"Controllers in
action"},
            {Name:"Models",Description :"Models and binding
data"},
            {Name:"Directives",Description :"Flexibility of
Directives"}
        ]});
</script>
</body>
</html>
```

Code Explanation:

1. We are first creating a variable called "tutorial" and assigning it

some key-value pairs in one step. Each key-value pair will be used as data when displaying the table. The tutorial variable is then assigned to the scope object so that it can be accessed from our view.

2. This is the first step in creating a table, and we use the <table> tag.

3. For each row of data, we are using the "ng-repeat directive". This directive goes through each key-value pair in the tuto,rial scope object by using the variable ptutor.

4. Finally, we are using the <td> tag along with the key-value pairs (ptutor.Name and ptutor.Description) to display the Angular table data.

If the code is executed successfully, the following Output will be shown when you run your code in the browser.

Output:

From the above output,

- We can see that the table is displayed properly with the data from

the array of key-value pairs defined in the controller.
- The table data was generated by going through each of the key-value pairs by using the "ng-repeat directive".

AngularJS in-built Filter

It's very common to use the inbuilt filters within AngularJS to change the way the data is displayed in the tables. We have already seen filters in action in an earlier chapter. Let's have a quick recap of filters before we proceed ahead.

In Angular.JS filters are used to format the value of expression before it is displayed to the user. An example of a filter is the 'uppercase' filter which takes on a string output and formats the string and displays all the characters in the string as uppercase.

So in the below example, if the value of the variable 'TutorialName' is 'AngularJS', the output of the below expression will be 'ANGULARJS'.

{{ TurotialName | uppercase }}

In this section, we will be looking at how the orderBy and uppercase filters can be used in tables in more detail.

Sort Table with OrderBy Filter

This filter is used to sort the table based on one of the table columns. In the previous example, the output for our Angular table data appeared as shown below.

Controllers	Controllers in action
Models	Models and binding data
Directives	Flexibility of Directives

Let's look at an example, on how we can use the "orderBy" filter and sort the Angular table data using the first column in the table.

```
<div ng-app="DemoApp" ng-controller="DemoController">
    <table >

        <tr ng-repeat="ptutor in tutorial | orderBy : 'Name'">

            <td>{{ ptutor.Name }}</td>
            <td>{{ ptutor.Description }}</td>

        </tr>
    </table>
</div>
<script type="text/javascript">
    var app = angular.module('DemoApp', []);
    app.controller('DemoController', function($scope) {

        $scope.tutorial ={
            {Name: "Controllers" , Description : "Controllers in action"},
            {Name: "Models" , Description : "Models and binding data"},
            {Name: "Directives" , Description : "Flexibility of Directives"}
        ]
    }
```

Using the orderBy clause.

```
<!DOCTYPE html>
<html>
<head>

    <meta chrset="UTF 8">

</head>
<body>
<title>Event Registration</title>
<style>
    table,th,td{
        border: 1px solid grey;
        padding:5px;
    }
</style>
<script src="https://code.angularjs.org/1.6.9/angular-route.js">
</script>
<script src="https://code.angularjs.org/1.6.9/angular.min.js">
</script>
<script src="https://code.angularjs.org/1.6.9/angular.js">
</script>
<script src="lib/bootstrap.js"></script>
<script src="lib/bootstrap.css"></script>

<h1> Guru99 Global Event</h1>

<div ng-app="DemoApp" ng-controller="DemoController">
    <table>
        <tr ng-repeat="ptutor in tutorial | orderBy : 'Name'">
            <td>{{ptutor.Name}}</td>
```

```
            <td>{{ptutor.Description}}</td>
        </tr>
    </table>
</div>

<script type="text/javascript">
    var app = angular.module('DemoApp',[]);

    app.controller('DemoController',function($scope) {

        $scope.tutorial = [
            {Name:"Controllers",Description :"Controllers in
action"},
            {Name:"Models",Description :"Models and binding
data"},
            {Name:"Directives",Description :"Flexibility of
Directives"}
        ]});
</script>
</body>
</html>
```

Code Explanation:

1. We are using the same code as we did for creating our table, the only difference this time is that we are using the "orderBy" filter along with the ng-repeat directive. In this case, we are saying that we want to order the table by the key "Name".

If the code is executed successfully, the following Output will be shown when you run your code in the browser.

Output:

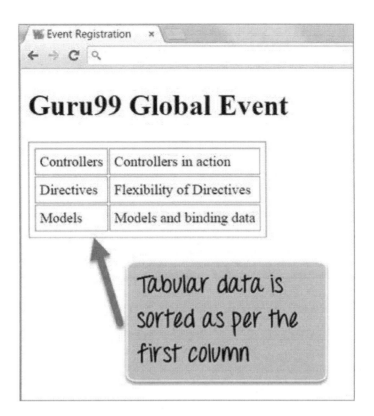

From the output,

- We can see that the data in the Angular table has been sorted as per the data in the first column. In our dataset, the "Directives" data comes from the "Models" data, but because we applied the orderBy filter, the tables get sorted accordingly.

Display Table with Uppercase Filter

We can also use the uppercase filter to change the data in the Angular table to uppercase.

Let's take a look at an example of how we can achieve this.

```
<div ng-app="DemoApp" ng-controller="DemoController">
    <table >

        <tr ng-repeat="ptutor in tutorial">

            <td>{{ ptutor.Name  | uppercase}}</td>

            <td>{{ ptutor.Description }}</td>

        </tr>
    </table>
</div>
<script type="text/javascript">
    var app = angular.module('DemoApp', []);
    app.controller('DemoController', function($scope) {

        $scope.tutorial =[
            {Name: "Controllers" , Description : "Controllers in action"},
            {Name: "Models" , Description : "Models and binding data"},
            {Name: "Directives" , Description : "Flexibility of Directives"}
        ]
```

> Using the uppercase filter

```
<!DOCTYPE html>
<html>
<head>

    <meta chrset="UTF 8">

</head>
<body>
<title>Event Registration</title>
<style>
    table,th,td{
        border: 1px solid grey;
        padding:5px;
    }
</style>
<script src="https://code.angularjs.org/1.6.9/angular-route.js">
</script>
<script src="https://code.angularjs.org/1.6.9/angular.min.js">
</script>
<script src="https://code.angularjs.org/1.6.9/angular.js">
</script>
<script src="lib/bootstrap.js"></script>
<script src="lib/bootstrap.css"></script>

<h1> Guru99 Global Event</h1>

<div ng-app="DemoApp" ng-controller="DemoController">
    <table>
```

```
        <tr ng-repeat="ptutor in tutorial">
            <td>{{ptutor.Name | uppercase}}</td>
            <td>{{ptutor.Description}}</td>
        </tr>
    </table>
</div>

<script type="text/javascript">
    var app = angular.module('DemoApp',[]);

    app.controller('DemoController',function($scope) {

        $scope.tutorial = [
            {Name:"Controllers",Description :"Controllers in
action"},
            {Name:"Models",Description :"Models and binding
data"},
            {Name:"Directives",Description :"Flexibility of
Directives"}
        ]});
</script>
</body>
</html>
```

Code Explanation:

1. We are using the same code as we did for creating our table, the only difference this time is that we are using the uppercase filter. We are using this filter in conjunction with the "ptutor.Name" so that all of the text in the first column will be displayed in uppercase.

If the code is executed successfully, the following Output will be shown when you run your code in the browser.

Output:

From the output,

- We can see that by using the "uppercase" filter, all of the data in the first column is displayed with uppercase characters.

Display the Table Index ($index)

To display the table index, add a <td> with $index.

Let's take a look at an example of how we can achieve this.

```
<div ng-app="DemoApp" ng-controller="DemoController">
    <table >

        <tr ng-repeat="ptutor in tutorial">

            <td>{{ $index + 1 }}</td>

            <td>{{ ptutor.Name }}</td>
            <td>{{ ptutor.Description }}</td>

        </tr>
    </table>
</div>
<script type="text/javascript">
    var app = angular.module('DemoApp', []);
    app.controller('DemoController', function($scope) {

        $scope.tutorial =[
            {Name: "Controllers" , Description : "Controllers in action"},
            {Name: "Models" , Description : "Models and binding data"},
            {Name: "Directives" , Description : "Flexibility of Directives"}
        ]
```

Adding an extra column and using the $index property

```
<!DOCTYPE html>
<html>
<head>

    <meta chrset="UTF 8">

</head>
<body>
<title>Event Registration</title>
<style>
    table,th,td{
        border: 1px solid grey;
        padding:5px;
    }
</style>
<script src="https://code.angularjs.org/1.6.9/angular-route.js">
</script>
<script src="https://code.angularjs.org/1.6.9/angular.min.js">
</script>
<script src="https://code.angularjs.org/1.6.9/angular.js">
</script>
<script src="lib/bootstrap.js"></script>
<script src="lib/bootstrap.css"></script>

<h1> Guru99 Global Event</h1>

<div ng-app="DemoApp" ng-controller="DemoController">
    <table>
        <tr ng-repeat="ptutor in tutorial">
            <td>{{$index + 1}}</td>
            <td>{{ptutor.Name}}</td>
```

```
            <td>{{ptutor.Description}}</td>
        </tr>
    </table>
</div>

<script type="text/javascript">
    var app = angular.module('DemoApp',[]);

    app.controller('DemoController',function($scope) {

        $scope.tutorial = [
            {Name:"Controllers",Description :"Controllers in
action"},
            {Name:"Models",Description :"Models and binding
data"},
            {Name:"Directives",Description :"Flexibility of
Directives"}
        ]});
</script>
</body>
</html>
```

Code Explanation:

1. We are using the same code as we did for creating our table, the
   only difference this time is that we are adding an extra row to our
   table to display the index column.

   In this additional column, we are using the "$index" property
   provided by AngularJS and then using the +1 operator to
   increment the index for each row.

If the code is executed successfully, the following Output will be shown
when you run your code in the browser.

Output:

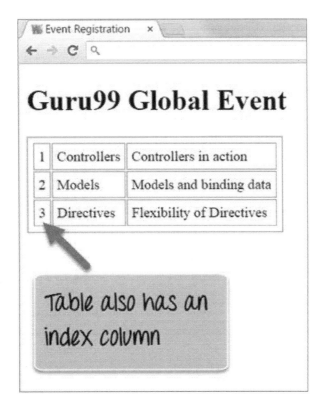

From the output,

- You can see that an additional column has been created. In this column, we can see the indexes being created for each row.

Summary:

- Table structures are created using the standard tags available within HTML. The data in the table is populated using the "ng-repeat" directive.
- The orderBy filter can be used to sort the table based on any column within the table.
- The uppercase filter can be used to display the data in any text-based column in uppercase.
- The "$index" property can be used to create an index for the table.
- One common issue encountered during development with AngularJS.JS tables is the implementation of large datasets which has 1000+ rows of data. Sometimes the ng-repeat directive can become non-responsive, and hence the entire page becomes unresponsive at times. In such a case, it always better to have

pagination in which the rows of data is spread across multiple pages.

Chapter 18: Form Validation

Validation is the process ensuring that data is correct and complete.

In a real-world example, let's assume a site which requires a registration form to be completed before getting full access to this site. The registration page would have input fields for username, password, email id and so forth.

When the user submits the form, normally a validation would occur first before the details are sent to the server. This validation would try to ensure to the best possible extent that the details for the input fields are entered in the right manner.

For example, the email id always needs to be in a format of **username@site.domain**; if someone enters just the username in the email id, then ideally the validation should fail. So validation looks at doing these basic checks before the details are sent to the server for further processing.

Form validation using HTML5

Form validation is the process of pre-validating information entered on a web form by the user before it is sent to the server. It's always better to validate the information on the client side itself. This is because it adds less overhead if the user had to be presented with the form again if the information entered was wrong.

Let's have a look at how form validation can be conducted in HTML5.

In our example, we will show one simple registration form to the user in which the user needs to enter details such as a username, password, email id, and age.

The form will have validation controls to ensure that the user enters the information in a proper manner.

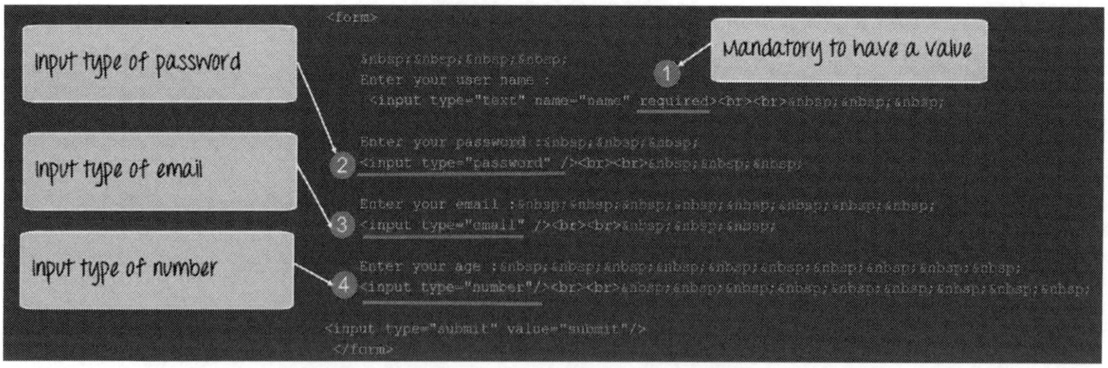

```
<!DOCTYPE html>
<html>
<head>

    <meta chrset="UTF 8">
    <title>Event Registration</title>
</head>

<body  ng-app="sampleApp">
<script src="https://code.angularjs.org/1.6.9/angular-route.js">
</script>
<script src="https://code.angularjs.org/1.6.9/angular.min.js">
</script>
<script src="https://code.angularjs.org/1.6.9/angular.js">
</script>
<script src="lib/bootstrap.js"></script>
<script src="lib/bootstrap.css"></script>
<h1> Guru99 Global Event</h1>
<div ng-controller="AngularController">

    <form>
            
        Enter your user name:
        <input type="text"  name="name" required><br>
<br>   

        Enter your password:   
        <input type="password"/><br><br>   

        Enter your
email:        
        <input type="email"/><br><br>   

        Enter your
age:         &
nbsp;
        <input type="number" /><br>
```

```
<br>         

        <input type="submit" value="Submit"/>
    </form>
</div>

</body>
</html>
```

Code Explanation:

1. For the text input type, we are using the 'required' attribute. This means that the textbox cannot be empty when the form is submitted, and some sort of text should be present in the textbox.
2. The next input type is password. Since the input type is marked as password, when the user enters any text in the field, it will be masked.
3. Because the input type is specified as email, the text in the box needs to match the pattern **name@site.domain**.
4. When the input type is marked as a number, if a user tries to enter any character using the keyboard or alphabet, it will not be entered in the textbox.

If the code is executed successfully, the following Output will be shown when you run your code in the browser.

Output:

To see the form validation in action, click the Submit button without entering any information on the screen.

After the submit button is clicked, a pop-up will come showing a validation error that the field needs to be filled.

So the validation for the control which was marked as required, causes the error message to be shown if the user does not enter any value in the text field.

When the user enters any value in the password control, you will notice the '*' symbol used to mask the characters being entered.

Let's then enter wrong email id and click the submit button. After the submit button is clicked, a pop-up will appear showing a validation error that the field needs to have the @ symbol.

So the validation for the control which was marked as an email control will cause the error message to be shown if the user does not enter a proper email id in the text field.

Finally, when you try to enter any characters in the age text control, it will not be entered on the screen. The control will only populate with a value when a number is entered in the control.

Form validation using $dirty, $valid, $invalid, $pristine

AngularJS provides its additional properties for validation. AngularJS provides the following properties for controls for validation purposes

- $dirty – The user has interacted with the control
- $valid – The field content is valid
- $invalid – The field content is invalid
- $pristine – The user has not interacted with the control as yet

Below are the steps which need to be followed to carry out Angular validation.

Step 1) Use the no validate property when declaring the form. This property tells HTML5 that the validation would be done by AngularJS.

Step 2) Ensure that the form has a name defined for it. The reason for doing this is that, when carrying out Angular validation, the form name will be used.

Step 3) Ensure each control also has a name defined for it. The reason for doing this is that, when carrying out Angular validation, the control name will be used.

Step 4) Use the ng-show directive to check for the $dirty, $invalid and

$valid properties for the controls.

Let's look at an example, which incorporates the above-mentioned steps.

In our example,

We are just going to have a simple text field in which the user needs to enter a Topic name in the text box. If this is not done, a validation error will be triggered, and the error message will be shown to the user.

```
<!DOCTYPE html>
<html>
<head>
    <meta chrset="UTF 8">
    <title>Event Registration</title>
</head>

<body>
<script src="https://code.angularjs.org/1.6.9/angular-route.js">
</script>
<script src="https://code.angularjs.org/1.6.9/angular.min.js">
</script>
<script src="https://code.angularjs.org/1.6.9/angular.js">
</script>
<script src="lib/bootstrap.js"></script>
<script src="lib/bootstrap.css"></script>
<h1> Guru99 Global Event</h1>
<form ng-app="DemoApp" ng-controller="DemoController"
name="myForm" novalidate>
    <p>Topic Name:<br>
        <input type="text" name="user" ng-model="user" required>

        <span style="color:red" ng-show="myForm.user.$dirty &&
```

```
myForm.user.$invalid">

            <span ng-show="myForm.user.$error.required">Username
is required</span>
        </span>
    </p>
    <p>
        <input type="submit" ng-disabled="myForm.user.$dirty &&
myForm.user.$invalid">
    </p>
</form>
<script>
    var app = angular.module("DemoApp",[]);

    app.controller("DemoController",function($scope) {

        $scope.Display = function () {
            $scope.user='Angular';
        }
    });
</script>
</body>
</html>
```

Code Explanation:

1. Note we have given a name for the Form which is "myForm". This is required when accessing the controls on the form for AngularJS validation.
2. Using the "novalidate" property for ensuring that the HTML form allows AngularJS to carry out the validation.
3. We are using the ng-show directive to check for the "$dirty" and "$invalid" property. This means that if the textbox has been modified, then the "$dirty" property value will be true. Also, in the case where the textbox value is null the "$invalid" property will become true. So if both properties are true, then the validation will fail for the control. Hence, if both values are true, the ng-show will also become true, and the span control with the red color characters will be displayed.
4. In this, we are checking the "$error" property which also evaluates to true because we have mentioned for the control that value

should be entered for the control. In such a case, where there is no data entered in the text box the span control will display the text "Username is required".

5. If the textbox control value is invalid, we also want to disable the submit button so that the user cannot submit the form. We are using the "ng-disabled" property for the control to do this based on the conditional value of the "$dirty" and "$invalid" property of the control.

6. In the controller, we are just setting the initial value of the textbox value to the text 'AngularJS'. This is just being done to set some default value to the textbox when the form is first displayed. It showcases better on how the validation occurs for the textbox field.

If the code is executed successfully, the following Output will be shown when you run your code in the browser.

Output:

When the form is initially displayed, the textbox displays the value of "AngularJS" and the "submit button" is enabled. As soon as you remove the text from the control, the validation error message is disabled, and the Submit button is disabled.

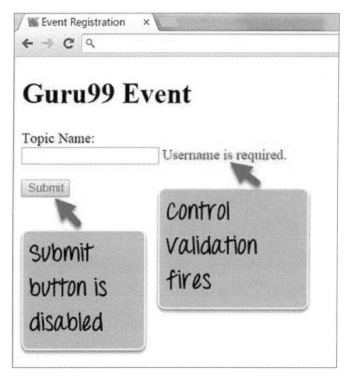

The above screenshot displays two things

- Submit button is disabled
- There is no topic name in Topic text box. Hence, it fires the error message "Username is required."

Form validation using AngularJS Auto Validate

There is a facility in AngularJS to have validated all controls on a form automatically without needing to write custom code for the validation. This can be done by including a custom module called "jcs-AutoValidate."

With this module in place, you don't need to place any special code to carry out the validation or show the error messages. This is all handled by the code inside of the JCS-AutoValidate.

Let's look at a simple example of how to achieve this.

In this example,

We are just going to have a simple form with a textbox control which is a required field. An error message should be displayed if this control is not filled in.

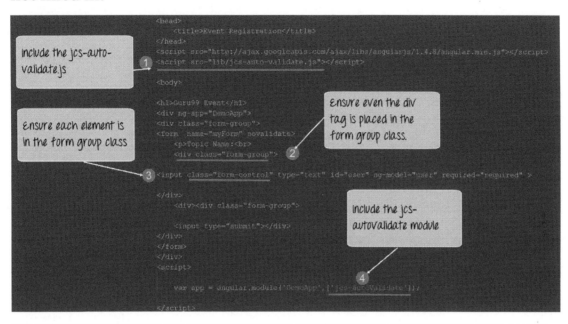

```
<!DOCTYPE html>
<html>
<head>
    <meta chrset="UTF 8">
    <title>Event Registration</title>
</head>
<script
src="https://ajax.googleapis.com/ajax/libs/angularjs/1.6.4/angula
r.min.js"></script>
<script src="https://code.angularjs.org/1.6.9/angular.js">
</script>
<script src="lib/jcs-auto-validate.min.js"></script>
<body>
<h1> Guru99 Event</h1>

<div ng-app="DemoApp">
    <div class="form-group">
        <form name="myForm" novalidate>
            <p>Topic Name:<br></p>
                <div class="form-group">
            <input class="form-control" type="text" id="user" ng-
model="user" required="required"/>

        </div>
```

```
            <div>
                <div class="form-group">
                    <input type="submit">
                </div>
            </div>
        </form>
    </div>
</div>
<script>
    var app=angular.module('DemoApp',['jcs-autoValidate']);
</script>
</body>
</html>
```

Code Explanation:

1. First, we need to include the "jcs-auto-validate.js" script which has all the auto validation functionality.
2. We need to ensure that each element including the "div tag" is placed in a "form-group" class.
3. Also need to ensure that each element (which is an HTML element such as input control, span control, div control and so on) such as the input controls are also placed in the form-group class.
4. Include the jcs-autovalidate in your AngularJS JS module.

If the code is executed successfully, the following Output will be shown when you run your code in the browser.

Output:

By default when you run your code the above form will be shown as per the HTML code.

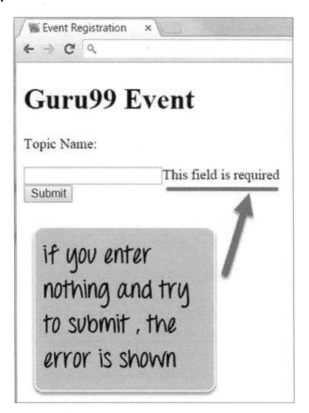

If you try to Submit the form, the error message will pop-up saying, "This field is required." All of this is done by the JCS-AutoValidate option.

User feedbacks with Ladda buttons

The "ladda" buttons is a special framework built for buttons on top of JavaScript to give a visual effect to buttons when they are pressed.

So if a button is given the "ladda" attribute and is pressed, a spin effect will be shown. Also, there are different data styles available for the button to provide additional visual effects.

Let's look at an example, of how to see "ladda" buttons in action. We are just going to see a simple form which has a submit button. When the button is pressed, a spin effect will be shown on the button.

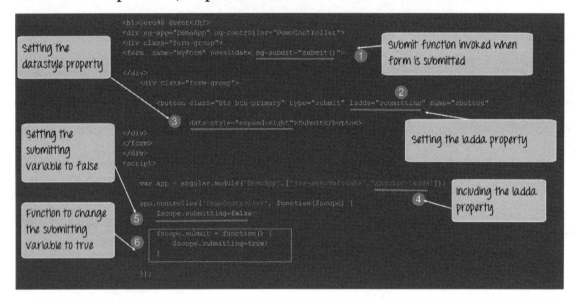

```
<!DOCTYPE html>
<html>
<head>
    <meta chrset="UTF 8">
    <title>Event Registration</title>
</head>
<script
src="https://ajax.googleapis.com/ajax/libs/angularjs/1.6.4/angula
r.min.js"></script>
<script src="https://code.angularjs.org/1.6.9/angular.js">
</script>
<script src="lib/jcs-auto-validate.min.js"></script>
<script src="lib/angular-ladda.js"></script>
<script src="lib/angular-ladda.min.js"></script>
<script src="lib/bootstrap.js"></script>
<script src="lib/bootstrap.css"></script>
```

```
<body>
<h1> Guru99 Event</h1>

<div ng-app="DemoApp" ng-controller="DemoController">
    <div class="form-group">
        <form name="myForm" novalidate ng-submit="submit()">
            <div>
                <button class="btn btn-primary" type="submit"
ladda="submitting" name="sbutton" data-style="expand-
right">Submit</button>
            </div>
        </form>
    </div>
</div>
<script>
    var app=angular.module('DemoApp',['jcs-
autoValidate','angular-ladda']);

    app.controller('DemoController',function($scope) {
        $scope.submitting = false;

        $scope.submit = function () {
            $scope.submitting = true;
        }
    });
</script>
</body>
</html>
```

Code Explanation:

1. We are using the "ng-submit" directive to call a function called
   "submit." This function will be used to change the ladda attribute
   of the submit button.

2. The ladda attribute is a special attribute of the ladda framework. It
   is this attribute which adds the spin effect to control. We are
   setting the value of the ladda attribute to the variable submitting.

3. The data-style property is again an additional attribute offered by
   the ladda framework, which just adds a different visual effect to
   the submit button.

4. The 'AngularJS-ladda' module needs to be added to the
   AngularJS.JS application in order for the ladda framework to
   work.

5. Initially, we are defining and setting the value of a variable called 'submitting' to false. This value is set for the ladda attribute of the submit button. By initially setting this to false we are saying that we don't want the submit button to have the ladda effect as of yet.

6. We are declaring a function which is called when the submit button is pressed. In this function, we are setting the 'submitting' to true. This will cause the ladda effect to be applied to the submit button.

If the code is executed successfully, the following Output will be shown when you run your code in the browser.

Output:

When the form is initially displayed, the submit button is shown in its simple form.

When the submit button is pressed, the submitting variable in the controller is set to true. This value gets passed to the "ladda" attribute of the submit button which causes the spin effect of the button.

Summary

- Validation for the textbox HTML controls can be done by using the 'required' attribute.
- In HTML5, there are new controls added such as password, email, and number which provide their own set of validations.
- Form validation in AngularJS is taken care of by looking at the $dirty, $valid, $invalid and $pristine values of a form control.
- Auto validation in AngularJS applications can also be achieved by using the JCS-auto validate module.
- Ladda buttons can be added to an Angular.js application to give a bit of an enhanced visual feel to the user when the button is pressed.

Chapter 19: Form Submit

How to Submit a form using ng-submit

The processes of submitting information on a web page are normally handled by the submit event on the web browser. This event is normally used to send information which the user might have entered on a web page to the server for further processing.

AngularJS also provides a directive called ng-submit which can be used to bind the application to the submit event of the browser.

So in the case of AngularJS, on the submit event you can carry out some processing within the controller itself and then display the processed information to the user.

Let's take an example of how we can achieve this.

In our example,

We are going to present a textbox to the user in which they can enter the topic which they want to learn. There will be a submit button on the page, which when pressed will add the topic to an unordered list.

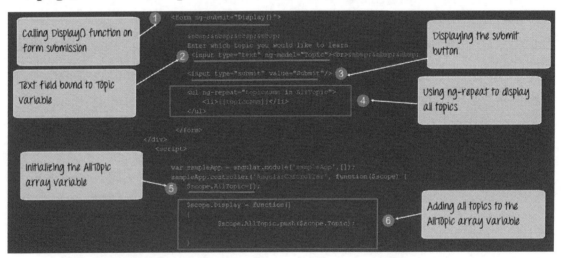

```
<!DOCTYPE html>
<html>
<head>
```

```
    <meta chrset="UTF 8">
    <title>Event Registration</title>
</head>

<body  ng-app="sampleApp">
<script src="https://code.angularjs.org/1.6.9/angular-route.js">
</script>
<script src="https://code.angularjs.org/1.6.9/angular.min.js">
</script>
<script src="https://code.angularjs.org/1.6.9/angular.js">
</script>
<script src="lib/bootstrap.js"></script>
<script src="lib/bootstrap.css"></script>
<h1> Guru99 Global Event</h1>
<div ng-controller="AngularController">

    <form ng-submit="Display()">
           
        Enter which topic you would like to learn
        <input type="text"  ng-app="sampleApp" ng-model="Topic">
<br>   

        <input type="submit" value="Submit"/>

        <ul ng-repeat="topicname in AllTopic">
            <li>{{topicname}}</li>
        </ul>
    </form>
</div>

<script>
    var app = angular.module("sampleApp",[]);

    app.controller("AngularController",function($scope) {

        $scope.Display = function () {
            $scope.AllTopic.push($scope.Topic);
        }
    });
</script>
</body>
</html>
```

Code Explanation:

1. We are first declaring our form HTML tag, which will hold the

"text box" and "submit button" control. We are then using the ng-submit directive to bind the function "Display()" to our form. This function will be defined in our controller and will be called when the form is submitted.

2. We have a text control in which the user will enter the Topic they want to learn. This will be bound to a variable called 'Topic' which will be used in our controller.

3. There is the normal submit button which the user will click when they have entered the topic they want.

4. We have used the ng-repeat directive to display list items of the topics the user enters. The ng-repeat directive goes through each topic in the array 'AllTopic' and displays the topic name accordingly.

5. In our controller, we are declaring an array variable called 'AllTopic.' This will be used to hold all the topics entered by the user in Step2.

6. We are defining the code for our Display() function which will be called whenever the user clicks the Submit button. Over here we are using the push array function to add the Topics entered by the user via the variable 'Topic' into our array 'AllTopic.'

If the code is executed successfully, the following Output will be shown when you run your code in the browser.

Output:

To see the code working, first, enter a Topic name like "AngularJS" as shown above in the textbox and then click on the Submit button.

- After the submit button is clicked, you will see the item which was entered in the textbox added to the list of items.
- This is being achieved by Display() function, which is called when

the submit button is pressed.

- The Display() function adds the text to the array variable called 'AllTopic.' And our ng-repeat directive goes through each value in the array variable 'AllTopic' and displays them as list items accordingly.

Summary

The "ng-submit" directive is used to process the input entered by the user when the form is submitted.

Chapter 20: ng-include

By default, HTML does not provide the facility to include client-side code from other files. It's normally a good practice in any programming language to distribute functionality across various files for any application.

For example, if you had logic for numeric operations, you would normally want to have that functionality defined in one separate file. That separate file could then be re-used across multiple applications by just including that file.

This is normally the concept of **Include statements** which are available in programming languages such as .Net and Java.

This tutorial looks at other ways files (files which contain external HTML code) can be included in the main HTML file.

Client Side includes

One of the most common ways is to include HTML code is via Javascript. JavaScript is a programming language which can be used to manipulate the content in an HTML page on the fly. Hence, Javascript can also be used to include code from other files.

The below steps shows how this can be accomplished.

Step1) Define a file called Sub.html and add the following code to the file.

```
<div>
        This is an included file
</div>
```

Step 2) Create a file called Sample.html, which is your main application file and add the below code snippet.

Below are the main aspects to note about the below code,

1. In the body tag, there is a div tag which has an id of Content. This is the place where the code from the external file 'Sub.html' will be inserted.
2. There is a reference to a jquery script. JQuery is a scripting language built on top of Javascript which makes DOM manipulation even easier.
3. In the Javascript function, there is a statement '$("#Content").load("Sub.html");' which causes the code in the file Sub.html to be injected in the div tag which has the id of Content.

```
<html>
        <head>
          <script src="jquery.js"></script>
          <script>
          $(function(){
            $("#Content").load("Sub.html");
          });
     </script>
   </head>

<body>
     <div id="Content"></div>
   </body>
</html>
```

Server Side Includes

Server Side Includes are also available for including a common piece of code throughout a site. This is normally done for including content in the below parts of an HTML document.

1. Page header
2. Page footer
3. Navigation menu.

For a web server to recognize a Server Side Includes, the file names have special extensions. They are usually accepted by the web server such as .shtml, .stm, .shtm , .cgi.

The directive used for including content is the "include directive". An example of the include directive is shown below;

```
<!--#include virtual="navigation.cgi" -->
```

- The above directive allows the content of one document to be included in another.
- The "virtual" command above code is used to specify the target relative to the domain root of the application.
- Also, to the virtual parameter, there is also the file parameter which can be used. The "file" parameters are used when one needs to specify the path relative to the directory of the current file.

Note:

The virtual parameter is used to specify the file (HTML page, text file, script, etc.) that needs to be included. If the web server process does not have access to read the file or execute the script, the include command will fail. The 'virtual' word is a keyword that is required to be placed in the include directive.

How to include HTML file in AngularJS

Angular provides the function to include the functionality from other AngularJS files by using the ng-include directive.

The primary purpose of the "ng-include directive" is used to fetch, compile and include an external HTML fragment in the main AngularJS application.

Let's look at the below code base and explain how this can be achieved using Angular.

Step 1) let's write the below code in a file called Table.html. This is the file which will be injected into our main application file using the ng-include directive.

The below code snippet assumes that there is a scope variable called "tutorial." It then uses the ng-repeat directive, which goes through each topic in the "Tutorial" variable and displays the values for the 'name' and 'description' key-value pair.

```
<table>
    <tr ng-repeat="Topic in tutorial">
        <td>{{ Topic.Name }}</td>
        <td>{{ Topic.Country }}</td>
    </tr>
</table>
```

Step 2) let's write the below code in a file called Main.html. This is a simple angular.JS application which has the following aspects

1. Use the "ng-include directive" to inject the code in the external file 'Table.html'. The statement has been highlighted in bold in the below code. So the div tag ' **<div ng-include="Table.html"> </div>**' will be replaced by the entire code in the 'Table.html' file.
2. In the controller, a "tutorial" variable is created as part of the $scope object. This variable contains a list of key-value pairs.

In our example, the key value pairs are

1. Name – This denotes the name of a topic such as Controllers, Models, and Directives.
2. Description – This gives a description of each topic

The tutorial variable is also accessed in the 'Table.html' file.

```
<!DOCTYPE html>
<html>
<head>
    <meta charset="UTF-8">
    <title>Event Registration</title>
        <script
src="http://ajax.googleapis.com/ajax/libs/angularjs/1.6.4/angular
.min.js"></script>
</head>
<body ng-app="sampleApp">
<div ng-controller="AngularController">
    <h3> Guru99 Global Event</h3>
```

```
                    <div ng-include="Table.html"></div>
</div>
<script>

    var sampleApp = angular.module('sampleApp',[]);
    sampleApp.controller('AngularController', function($scope) {
        $scope.tutorial =[
            {Name: "Controllers" , Description : "Controllers in
action"},
            {Name: "Models" , Description : "Models and binding
data"},
            {Name: "Directives" , Description : "Flexibility of
Directives"}
        ];


    });
</script>
</body>
</html>
```

When you execute the above code, you will get the following output.

Output:

Gur99 Global Event

Controllers	Controllers in action
Models	Models and binding data
Directives	Flexibility of Directives

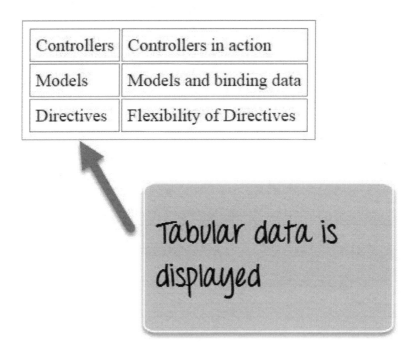

Tabular data is displayed

Summary:

- By default, we know that HTML does not provide a direct way to include HTML content from other files like other programming languages.
- Javascript along with JQuery is the best-preferred option for embedding HTML content from other files.
- Another way of including HTML content from other files is to use the <include> directive and the virtual parameter keyword. The virtual parameter keyword is used to denote the file which needs to be embedded. This is known as server-side includes.
- Angular also provides the facility to include files by using the ng-include directive. This directive can be used to inject code from external files directly into the main HTML file.

Chapter 21: Dependency Injection

What is Dependency Injection in AngularJS?

Dependency Injection is a software design pattern that implements inversion of control for resolving dependencies.

Inversion of Control: It means that objects do not create other objects on which they rely to do their work. Instead, they get these objects from an outside source. This forms the basis of dependency injection wherein if one object is dependent on another; the primary object does not take the responsibility of creating the dependent object and then use its methods. Instead, an external source (which in AngularJS, is the AngularJS framework itself) creates the dependent object and gives it to the source object for further usage.

So let's first understand what a dependency is.

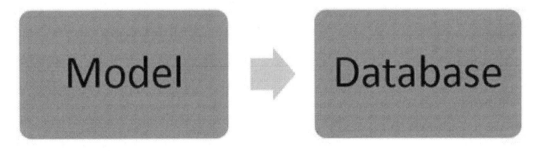

The above diagram shows a simple example of an everyday ritual in database programming.

- The 'Model' box depicts the "Model class" which is normally created to interact with the database. So now the database is a dependency for the "Model class" to function.
- By dependency injection, we create a service to grab all the

information from the database and get into the model class.

In the remainder of this tutorial, we will look more at dependency injection and how this is accomplished in AngularJS.

Which Component can be Injected as a Dependency In AngularJS

In Angular.JS, dependencies are injected by using an "injectable factory method" or "constructor function".

These components can be injected with "service" and "value" components as dependencies. We have seen this in an earlier topic with the $http service.

We've already seen that the $http service can be used within AngularJS to get data from a MySQL or MS SQL Server database via a PHP web application.

The $http service is normally defined from within the controller in the following manner.

```
  sampleApp.controller ('AngularJSController', function ($scope,
$http)
```

Now when the $http service is defined in the controller as shown above. It means that the controller now has a dependency on the $http service.

So when the above code gets executed, AngularJS will perform the following steps;

1. Check to see if the "$http service" has been instantiated. Since our "controller" now depends on the "$http service", an object of this service needs to be made available to our controller.
2. If AngularJS finds out that the $http service is not instantiated, AngularJS uses the 'factory' function to construct an $http object.
3. The injector within Angular.JS then provides an instance of the

$http service to our controller for further processing.

Now that the dependency is injected into our controller, we can now invoke the necessary functions within the $http service for further processing.

Example of Dependency Injection

Dependency injection can be implemented in 2 ways

1. One is through the "Value Component"
2. Another is through a "Service"

Let's look at the implementation of both ways in more detail.

1) Value component

This concept is based on the fact of creating a simple JavaScript object and pass it to the controller for further processing.

This is implemented using the below two steps

Step 1) Create a JavaScript object by using the value component and attach it to your main AngularJS.JS module.

The value component takes on two parameters; one is the key, and the other is the value of the javascript object which is created.

Step 2) Access the JavaScript object from the Angular.JS controller

```
<! DOCTYPE html>
<html>
<head>
    <meta charset="UTF-8">
    <title>Event Registration</title>

</head>
<script
src="https://ajax.googleapis.com/ajax/libs/angularjs/1.6.4/angula
r.min.js"></script>
<body ng-app="sampleApp">
```

```
<div ng-controller="AngularJSController">
    <h3> Guru99 Global Event</h3>
    {{ID}}
</div>
<script>

    var sampleApp = angular.module('sampleApp',[]);
    sampleApp.value("TutorialID", 5);
    sampleApp.controller('AngularJSController',
function($scope,TutorialID) {
        $scope.ID =TutorialID;
    });

</script>
</body>
</html>
```

In the above code example, the below main steps are being carried out

1. `sampleApp.value("TutorialID", 5);`

The value function of the Angular.JS JS module is being used to create a key-value pair called "TutorialID" and the value of "5".

2. `sampleApp.controller('AngularJSController', function ($scope,TutorialID)`

The TutorialID variable now becomes accessible to the controller as a function parameter.

3. `$scope.ID =TutorialID;`

The value of TutorialID which is 5, is now being assigned to another variable called ID in the $scope object. This is being done so that value of 5 can be passed from the controller to the view.

4. `{{ID}}`

The ID parameter is being displayed in the view as an expression. So the output of '5' will be displayed on the page.

When the above code is executed, the output will be shown as below

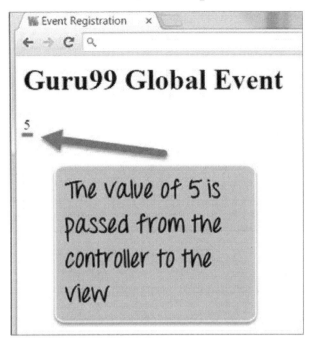

2) Service

Service is defined as a singleton JavaScript object consisting of a set of functions that you want to expose and inject in your controller.

For example, the "$http" is a service in Angular.JS which when injected in your controllers provides the necessary functions of

(get() , query() , save() , remove(), delete()).

These functions can then be invoked from your controller accordingly.

Let's look at a simple example of how you can create your own service. We are going to create a simple addition service which adds two numbers.

```html
<! DOCTYPE html>
<html>
<head>
    <meta charset="UTF-8">
    <title>Event Registration</title>

</head>
<script
```

```
src="https://ajax.googleapis.com/ajax/libs/angularjs/1.6.4/angula
r.min.js"></script>
<body>
<h3> Guru99 Global Event</h3>

<div ng-app = "mainApp" ng-controller = "DemoController">
    <p>Result: {{result}}</p>
</div>
<script>
    var mainApp = angular.module("mainApp", []);

    mainApp.service('AdditionService', function(){
        this.ADDITION = function(a,b) {
            return a+b;
        }
    });

    mainApp.controller('DemoController', function($scope,
AdditionService) {

            $scope.result = AdditionService.ADDITION(5,6);
    });
</script>

</body>
</html>
```

In the above example, the following steps are carried out

1. ```
mainApp.service('AdditionService', function()
```

Here we are creating a new service called 'AdditionService' using the service parameter of our main AngularJS JS module.

2. ```
this.Addition = function(a,b)
```

Here we are creating a new function called Addition within our service. This means that when AngularJS instantiates our AdditionService inside of our controller, we would then be able to access the 'Addition' function. In this function definition, we are saying that this function accepts two parameters, a and b.

3. ```
return a+b;
```
```

Here we are defining the body of our Addition function which simply adds the parameters and returns the added value.

4.
```
mainApp.controller('DemoController', function($scope,
AdditionService)
```

This is the main step which involves dependency injection. In our controller definition, we are now referencing our 'AdditionService' service. When AngularJS see's this, it will instantiate an object of type 'AdditionService.'

5.
```
$scope.result = AdditionService.Addition(5,6);
```

We are now accessing the function 'Addition' which is defined in our service and assigning it to the $scope object of the controller.

So this is a simple example of how we can define our service and inject the functionality of that service inside of our controller.

Summary:

- Dependency Injection as the name implies is the process of injecting dependent functionality into modules at run time.
- Using dependency injection helps in having a more re-usable code. If you had common functionality that is used across multiple application modules, the best way is to define a central service with that functionality and then inject that service as a dependency in your application modules.
- The value object of AngularJS can be used to inject simple JavaScript objects in your controller.
- The service module can be used to define your custom services which can be re-used across multiple AngularJS modules.

Chapter 22: Karma Jasmine

One of the most brilliant features of Angular.JS is the Testing aspect. When the developers at Google developed AngularJS, they kept testing in mind and made sure that the entire AngularJS framework was testable.

In AngularJS, testing is normally carried out using Karma (framework). Angular JS testing can be carried out without Karma, but the Karma framework has such a brilliant functionality for testing AngularJS code, that it makes sense to use this framework.

- In AngularJS, we can perform Unit Testing separately for controllers and directives.
- We can also perform end of end testing of AngularJS, which is testing from a user perspective.

Introduction & Installation of Karma framework

Karma is a testing automation tool created by the Angular JS team at Google. The first step for using Karma is to install Karma. Karma is installed via npm (which is a package manager used for easy installation of modules on a local machine).

Installation of Karma

The installation of Karma via npm is done in a two steps process.

Step 1) Execute the below line from within the command line

```
npm install karma karma-chrome-launcher karma-jasmine
```

Wherein

1. npm is the command line utility for the node package manager used for installing custom modules on any machine.
2. The install parameter instructs the npm command line utility that installation is required.
3. There are 3 libraries being specified in the command line that are required to work with karma
   - karma is the core library which will be used for testing purposes.
   - karma-chrome-launcher is a separate library which enables karma commands to be recognized by the chrome browser.
   - karma-jasmine – This installs jasmine which is a dependent framework for Karma.

Step 2) The next step is to install the karma command line utility. This is required for executing karma line commands. The karma line utility will be used to initialize the karma environment for testing.

To install the command line utility execute the below line from within the command line

```
npm install karma-cli
```

wherein,

1. karma-cli is used to install the command line interface for karma which will be used to write the karma commands in the command line interface.

Configuration of the Karma framework

The next step is to configure karma which can be done via the command

```
"karma -init"
```

After the above step is executed, karma will create a karma.conf.js file. The file will probably look like the snippet shown below

```
files: [
  'Your application Name'/AngularJS/AngularJS.js',
  'Your application Name'/AngularJS-mocks/AngularJS-mocks.js',
  'lib/app.js',
  'tests/*.js'
]
```

The above configuration files tell the karma runtime engine the following things

1. **'Your application Name'** – This will be replaced by the name of your application.

2. **'Your application Name'/AngularJS/AngularJS.js'** – This tells karma that your application depends on the core modules in AngularJS

3. **'Your application Name'/AngularJS-mocks/AngularJS-mocks.js'** – This tells karma to use the Unit Testing functionality for AngularJS from the Angular.JS-mocks.js file.

4. All of the main application or business logic files are present in the lib folder of your application.

5. The tests folder will contain all of the unit tests

To check if karma is working, create a file called Sample.js, put in the below code and place it in the test directory.

```
describe('Sample test', function() {
  it('Condition is true', function() {
    expect('AngularJS').toBe('AngularJS');
  });
});
```

The above code has the following aspects

1. The describe function is used to give a description of the test. In our case, we are giving the description 'Sample test' to our test.

2. The 'it' function is used to give a name to the test. In our case, we are giving the name of our test as 'Condition is true'. The name of the test needs to be meaningful.

3. The combination of the 'expect' and 'toBe' keyword states on what

is the expected and actual value of the test result. If the actual and expected value is the same, then the test will pass else it will fail.

When you execute the following line at the command prompt, it will execute the above test file

```
KARMA start
```

The below output is taken from the IDE Webstorm in which the above steps were carried out.

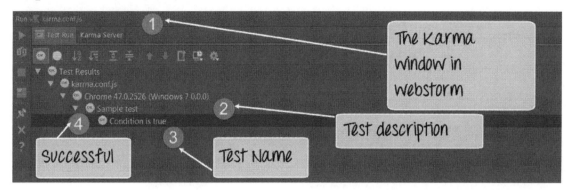

1. The output comes in the Karma explorer within Webstorm. This window shows the execution of all tests which are defined in the karma framework.
2. Here you can see that the description of the test executed is shown which is "Sample test."
3. Next, you can see that the test itself which has a name of "Condition is true" is executed.
4. Note that since all tests have the green "Ok" icon next to it which symbolizes that all tests passed.

Testing AngularJS Controllers

The karma testing framework also has the functionality to test Controllers end to end. This includes testing of the $scope object which is used within Controllers.

Let's look at an example of how we can achieve this.

In our example,

We would first need to define a controller. This controller would carry out the below-mentioned steps

1. Create an ID variable and assign the value 5 to it.
2. Assign the ID variable to the $scope object.

Our test will test the existence of this controller and also test to see if the ID variable of the $scope object is set to 5.

First we need to ensure the following pre-requisite is in place

1. Install the Angular.JS-mocks library via npm. This can be done by executing the below line in the command prompt

```
npm install Angular JS-mocks
```

1. Next is to modify the karma.conf.js file to ensure the right files are included for the test. The below segment just shows the files part of the karma.conf.js which needs to be modified

```
files: ['lib/AngularJS.js','lib/AngularJS-
mocks.js','lib/index.js','test/*.js']
```

- The 'files' parameter basically tells Karma all the files that are required in the running of the tests.
- The AngularJS.js and AngularJS-mocks.js file are required to run AngularJS unit tests
- The index.js file is going to contain our code for the controller
- The test folder is going to contain all our AngularJS tests

Below is our Angular.JS code which will be stored as a file Index.js in the test folder of our application.

The below code just does the following things

1. Create an Angular JS module called sampleApp
2. Create a controller called AngularJSController
3. Create a variable called ID, give it a value of 5 and assign it to the $scope object

```
var sampleApp = AngularJS.module('sampleApp',[]);
sampleApp.controller('AngularJSController', function($scope) {
    $scope.ID =5;
});
```

Once the above code is executed successfully, the next step would be to create a Test Case to ensure the code has been written and executed properly.

The code for our test will be as shown below.

The code will be in a separate file called ControllerTest.js, which will be placed in the test folder. The below code just does the following key things

1. beforeEach function – This function is used to load our AngularJS.JS module called 'sampleApp' before the test run. Note that this is the name of the module in an index.js file.

2. The $controller object is created as a mockup object for the controller "Angular JSController" which is defined in our index.js file. In any sort of Unit Testing, a mock object represents a dummy object which will actually be used for the testing. This mock object will actually simulate the behavior of our controller.

3. beforeEach(inject(function(_$controller_) – This is used to inject the mock object in our test so that it behaves like the actual controller.

4. var $scope = {}; This is a mock object being created for the $scope object.

5. var controller = $controller('AngularJSController', { $scope: $scope }); - Here we are checking for the existence of a controller named 'Angular.JSController'. In here we are also assigning all variables from our $scope object in our controller in the Index.js file to the $scope object in our test file

6. Finally, we are comparing the $scope.ID to 5

```
describe('AngularJSController', function() {
```

```
    beforeEach(module('sampleApp'));

    var $controller;

    beforeEach(inject(function(_$controller_){
            $controller = _$controller_;
    }));

    describe('$scope.ID', function() {
        it('Check the scope object', function() {
            var $scope = {};
            var controller = $controller('AngularJSController', {
$scope: $scope });
            expect($scope.ID).toEqual(5);
        });
    });
});
```

The above test will run in the karma browser and give the same pass result as was shown in the previous topic.

Testing AngularJS Directives

The karma testing framework also has the functionality to test custom directives. This includes the templateURL's which are used within custom directives.

Let's look at an example of how we can achieve this.

In our example, we will first define a custom directive which does the following things

1. Create an AngularJS module called sampleApp
2. Create a custom directive with the name – Guru99
3. Create a function that returns a template with a header tag which displays the text "This is AngularJS Testing."

```
var sampleApp = AngularJS.module('sampleApp',[]);
sampleApp.directive('Guru99', function () {
    return {
        restrict: 'E',
        replace: true,
        template: '<h1>This is AngularJS Testing</h1>'
```

```
    };
});
```

Once the above code is executed successfully, the next step would be to create a test case to ensure the code has been written and executed properly. The code for our test will be as shown below

The code will be in a separate file called DirectiveTest.js, which will be placed in the test folder. The below code just does the following key things

1. beforeEach function – This function is used to load our Angular JS module called 'sampleApp' before the test run.

2. The $compile service is used to compile the directive. This service is mandatory and needs to be declared so that Angular.JS can use it to compile our custom directive.

3. The $rootscope is the primary scope of any AngularJS.JS application. We have seen the $scope object of the controller in earlier chapters. Well, the $scope object is the child object of the $rootscope object. The reason this is declared here is because we are making a change to an actual HTML tag in the DOM via our custom directive. Hence, we need to use the $rootscope service which actually listens or knows when any change happens from within an HTML document.

4. var element = $compile("<ng-Guru99></ng-Guru99>") – This is used to check whether our directive gets injected as it should. The name of our custom directive is Guru99, and we know from our custom directives chapter that when the directive is injected in our HTML, it will be injected as '<ng-Guru99></ng-Guru99>'. Hence this statement is used to make that check.

5. expect(element.html()).toContain("This is AngularJS Testing") – This is used to instruct the expect function that it should find the element(in our case the div tag) to contain the innerHTML text of "This is AngularJS Testing".

```
describe('Unit testing directives', function() {
  var $compile,
      $rootScope;
   beforeEach(module('sampleApp'));

   beforeEach(inject(function(_$compile_, _$rootScope_){
     $compile = _$compile_;
     $rootScope = _$rootScope_;
 }));

   it('Check the directive', function() {
     // Compile a piece of HTML containing the directive
     var element = $compile("<ng-Guru99></ng-Guru99>")
($rootScope);
     $rootScope.$digest();
     expect(element.html()).toContain("This is AngularJS
Testing");
   });
});
```

The above test will run in the karma browser and give the same pass result as was shown in the previous topic.

End to End Testing AngularJS JS applications

The karma testing framework along with a framework called Protractor has the functionality of testing a web application end to end.

So it's not only testing of directives and controllers, but also testing of anything else which may appear on an HTML page.

Let's look at an example of how we can achieve this.

In our example below, we are going to have an AngularJS application which creates a data table using the ng-repeat directive.

1. We are first creating a variable called "tutorial" and assigning it some key-value pairs in one step. Each key-value pair will be used as data when displaying the table. The tutorial variable is then assigned to the scope object so that it can be accessed from our

view.

2. For each row of data in the table, we are using the ng-repeat directive. This directive goes through each key-value pair in the tutorial scope object by using the variable ptutor.

3. Finally, we are using the <td> tag along with the key value pairs (ptutor.Name and ptutor.Description) to display the table data.

```
<table >
            <tr ng-repeat="ptutor in tutorial">
                <td>{{ ptutor.Name }}</td>
                    <td>{{ ptutor.Description }}</td>
            </tr>
    </table>
</div>
  <script type="text/javascript">
      var app = AngularJS.module('DemoApp', []);
        app.controller('DemoController', function($scope) {
          $scope.tutorial =[
              {Name: "Controllers" , Description : "Controllers
in action"},
              {Name: "Models" , Description : "Models and
binding data"},
                {Name: "Directives" , Description :
"Flexibility of Directives"}
                    ]   });
```

Once the above code is executed successfully, the next step would be to create a test case to ensure the code has been written and executed properly. The code for our test will be as shown below

Our test is actually going to test the ng-repeat directive and ensure that it contains 3 rows of data as it should from the above example.

First we need to ensure the following pre-requisite is in place

1. Install the protractor library via npm. This can be done by executing the below line in the command prompt

```
"npm install protractor"
```

The code for our test will be as shown below.

The code will be in a separate file called CompleteTest.js , which will be placed in the test folder. The below code just does the following key things

1. The browser function is provided by the protractor library and assumes that our AngularJS application (with the code shown above) is running on our site URL - http://localhost:8080/Guru99/

2. var list=element.all(by.repeater(ptutor in tutorial')); -

   This line of code is actually fetching the ng-repeat directive which is populated by the code 'ptutor in tutorial'. The element and by.repeater are special keywords provided by the protractor library that allows us to get details of the ng-repeat directive.

3. expect(list.count()).toEqual(3); - Lastly, we are using the expect function to see that we are indeed getting 3 items being populated in our table as a result of the ng-repeat directive.

```
Describe('Unit testing end to end', function() {
  beforeEach(function() {
browser.get('http://localhost:8080/Guru99/');
})
   it('Check the ng directive', function() {
      var list=element.all(by.repeater(ptutor in tutorial'));
      expect(list.count()).toEqual(3);   }); });
```

The above test will run in the karma browser and give the same pass result as was shown in the previous topic.

Summary

- Testing in AngularJS is achieved by using the karma framework, a framework which has been developed by Google itself.
- The karma framework is installed using the node package manager. The key modules which are required to be installed for basic testing are karma, karma-chrome-launcher ,karma-jasmine, and karma-cli.
- The tests are written in separate js files, normally kept in the test folder of your application. The location of these test files must be

mentioned in a special configuration file called karma.conf.js. Karma uses this configuration file when executing all tests.

- Karma can be used to test Controllers and custom directives as well.
- For an end to end web testing, another framework called protractor needs to be installed via the Node, package manager. This framework provides special methods which can be used to test all of the elements on an HTML page.

Chapter 23: Protractor Testing

Protractor plays an important role in the Testing of AngularJS applications and works as a Solution integrator combining powerful technologies like Selenium, Jasmine, Web driver, etc. It is intended not only to test AngularJS application but also for writing automated regression tests for normal Web Applications as well.

Why Do We Need Protractor Framework?

JavaScript is used in almost all web applications. As the applications grow, JavaScript also increases in size and complexity. In such case, it becomes a difficult task for Testers to test the web application for various scenarios.

Sometimes it is difficult to capture the web elements in AngularJS applications using JUnit or Selenium WebDriver.

Protractor is a NodeJS program which is written in JavaScript and runs with Node to identify the web elements in AngularJS applications, and it also uses WebDriver to control the browser with user actions.

Ok, fine now let's discuss what exactly is an AngularJS application?

AngularJS applications are Web Applications which uses extended HTML's syntax to express web application components. It is mainly used for dynamic web applications. These applications use less and flexible code compared with normal Web Applications.

Why can't we find Angular JS web elements using Normal Selenium Web driver?

Angular JS applications have some extra HTML attributes like ng-repeater, ng-controller, ng-model.., etc. which are not included in Selenium locators. Selenium is not able to identify those web elements using Selenium code. So, Protractor on the top of Selenium can handle and controls those attributes in Web Applications.

The protractor is an end to end testing framework for Angular JS based applications. While most frameworks focus on conducting unit tests for Angular JS applications, Protractor focuses on testing the actual functionality of an application.

Before we start Protractor, we need to install the following:

1. Selenium

   You can find the Selenium Installation steps in the following links, (https://www.guru99.com/installing-selenium-webdriver.html)

2. NPM (Node.js)

   NodeJS Installation, we need to install NodeJS to install Protractor. You can find this installation steps in the following link. (https://www.guru99.com/download-install-node-js.html)

Protractor Installation

Step 1) Open command prompt and type **"npm install –g protractor"** and hit Enter.

The above command will download the necessary files and install Protractor on the client system.

Step 2) Check the installation and version using **"Protractor — version."** If successful it will show the version as like in below screenshot. If not, perform the step 1 again.

```
C:\Users\RE041943>protractor --version
Version 3.1.1
```

(Steps 3 and 4 are Optional but recommended for better practice)

Step 3) Update the Web driver manager. The web driver manager is used for running the tests against the angular web application in a specific browser. After Protractor is installed, the web driver manager needs to be updated to the latest version. This can be done by running the following command in the command prompt.

```
webdriver-manager update
```

```
C:\Users\RE041943>webdriver-manager update
Updating selenium standalone
downloading https://selenium-release.storage.googleapis.com/2.51/selenium-server
-standalone-2.51.0.jar...
Updating chromedriver
downloading https://chromedriver.storage.googleapis.com/2.21/chromedriver_win32.
zip...
chromedriver_2.21.zip downloaded to C:\Users\RE041943\AppData\Roaming\npm\node_m
odules\protractor\selenium\chromedriver_2.21.zip
selenium-server-standalone-2.51.0.jar downloaded to C:\Users\RE041943\AppData\Ro
aming\npm\node_modules\protractor\selenium\selenium-server-standalone-2.51.0.jar
```

Step 4) Start the web driver manager. This step will run the web driver manager in the background and will listen to any tests which run via protractor.

Once Protractor is used to run any test, the web driver will automatically load and run the test in the relevant browser. To start the web driver manager, the following command needs to be executed from the command prompt.

```
webdriver-manager start
```

```
C:\Users\RE041943>webdriver-manager start
seleniumProcess.pid: 3168
18:13:36.624 INFO - Launching a standalone Selenium Server
Setting system property webdriver.chrome.driver to C:\Users\RE041943\AppData\F
18:13:37.531 INFO - Java: Oracle Corporation 25.51-b03
18:13:37.534 INFO - OS: Windows 7 6.1 amd64
18:13:37.659 INFO - v2.51.0, with Core v2.51.0. Built from revision 1af067d
18:13:37.903 INFO - Driver class not found: com.opera.core.systems.OperaDriver
18:13:37.904 INFO - Driver provider com.opera.core.systems.OperaDriver is not
18:13:37.929 INFO - Driver provider org.openqa.selenium.safari.SafariDriver re
registration capabilities Capabilities [{browserName=safari, version=, platfor
18:13:39.631 INFO - RemoteWebDriver instances should connect to: http://127.0.
18:13:39.635 INFO - Selenium Server is up and running
```

Now, if you go to the following URL
(**http://localhost:4444/wd/hub/static/resource/hub.html**) in
your browser, you will actually see the Web driver manager running in
the background.

Sample AngularJS application testing using Protractor

Protractor needs two files to run, a **spec** file and **configuration** file.

1. **Configuration file**: This File helps protractor to where the test
   files are placed (specs.js) and to talk with Selenium server
   (Selenium Address). Chrome is the default browser for Protractor.

2. **Spec file:** This File contains the logic and locators to interact
   with the application.

Step 1) We have to login https://angularjs.org and enter the text as
"GURU99" in "Enter a name here" textbox.

Step 2) In this step,

1. Entered the name "Guru99"
2. In output text " Hello Guru99" is seen.

Step 3) Now we have to capture the text from the webpage after entering the name and need to verify with the expected text.

Code:

We have to prepare configuration file **(conf.js)** and spec file **(spec.js)** as mentioned above.

Logic of spec.js :

```
describe('Enter GURU99 Name', function() {
 it('should add a Name as GURU99', function() {
 browser.get('https://angularjs.org');
 element(by.model('yourName')).sendKeys('GURU99');
   var guru=
element(by.xpath('html/body/div[2]/div[1]/div[2]/div[2]/div/h1'))
;
expect(guru.getText()).toEqual('Hello GURU99!');
   });
});
```

Code Explanation of spec.js:

1. **describe**('Enter GURU99 Name', function()

   The describe syntax is from the Jasmine framework. Here "describe" ('Enter GURU99 Name') typically defines components of an application, which can be a class or function etc. In the code suite called as "Enter GURU99," it's just a string and not a code.

2. **it**('should add a Name as GURU99', function()

3. **browser.get**('https://angularjs.org')

   As like in Selenium Webdriver browser.get will open a new browser instance with mentioned URL.

4. **element**(by.model('yourName')).**sendKeys**('GURU99')

   Here we are finding the web element using the Model name as "yourName," which is the value of "ng-model" on the web page. Check the screen shot below-

5. var guru= element(by.xpath('html/body/div[2]/div[1]/div[2]/div[2]/div/h1')

   Here we are finding the web element using XPath and store its value in a variable "guru".

6. **expect**(guru.getText()).**toEqual**('Hello GURU99!')

   Finally we are verifying the text which we have got from the webpage (using gettext()) with expected text .

Logic of conf.js:

```
exports.config = {
  seleniumAddress: 'http://localhost:4444/wd/hub',
  specs: ['spec.js']
};
```

Code Explanation of conf.js

1. seleniumAddress: 'http://localhost:4444/wd/hub'

   The Configuration file tells Protractor the location of Selenium Address to talk with Selenium WebDriver.

2. specs: ['spec.js']

   This line tells Protractor the location of test files spec.js

Execution of the Code

Here first, we will change the directory path or navigate to the folder where the confi.js and spec.js are placed in our system.

Follow the following step.

Step 1) Open the command prompt.

Step 2) Make sure selenium web driver manager is up and running. For that give the command as "webdriver-manager start" and hit Enter.

```
C:\Users\RE041943>webdriver-manager start
seleniumProcess.pid= 3468
18:13:36.624 INFO - Launching a standalone Selenium Server
Setting system property webdriver.chrome.driver to C:\Users\RE041943\AppData\Roaming\npm\node_
18:13:37.531 INFO - Java: Oracle Corporation 25.51-b03
18:13:37.534 INFO - OS: Windows 7 6.1 amd64
18:13:37.659 INFO - v2.51.0, with Core v2.51.0. Built from revision 1af067d
18:13:37.903 INFO - Driver class not found: com.opera.core.systems.OperaDriver
18:13:37.904 INFO - Driver provider com.opera.core.systems.OperaDriver is not registered
18:13:37.929 INFO - Driver provider org.openqa.selenium.safari.SafariDriver registration is sk
registration capabilities Capabilities [{browserName=safari, version=, platform=MAC}] does not
18:13:39.631 INFO - RemoteWebDriver instances should connect to: http://127.0.0.1:4444/wd/hub
18:13:39.635 INFO - Selenium Server is up and running
```

(If selenium web driver is not up and running we cannot proceed with a test as Protractor cannot find the web driver to handle the web application)

Step 3) Open a new command prompt and give the command as **"protractor conf.js"** to run the configuration file.

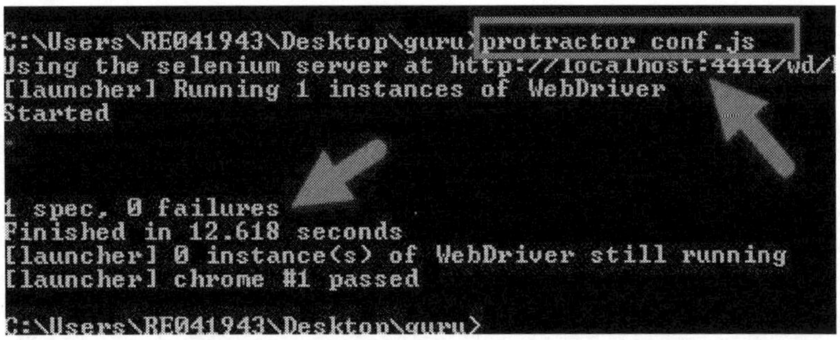

Explanation:

- Here Protractor will execute the configuration file with given spec file in it.
- We can see the selenium server running at **"http://localhost:4444/wd/hub"** which we have given in the conf.js file.
- Also, here can see the result how many are passed and failures like in above screenshot.

Fine, we have verified the result when it is passed or as expected. Now let us look into fail result also.

Step 1) Open and change expected to result in spec.js to "'Hello change GURU99" like below.

After change in spec.js :

```
describe('Enter GURU99 Name', function() {
 it('should add a Name as GURU99', function() {
 browser.get('https://angularjs.org');
 element(by.model('yourName')).sendKeys('GURU99');
  var guru=
element(by.xpath('html/body/div[2]/div[1]/div[2]/div[2]/div/h1'))
;
expect(guru.getText()).toEqual('Hello change GURU99!');
  });
});
```

Step 2) Save the spec.js file and repeat above steps of "Execution of the Code" section

Now, execute the above steps.

Result:

```
C:\Users\RE041943\Desktop\guru>protractor conf.js
Using the selenium server at http://localhost:4444/wd/hub
[launcher] Running 1 instances of WebDriver
Started

Failures:
1) Enter GURU99 Name should add a Name as GURU99
Message:
    Expected 'Hello GURU99!' to equal 'Hello change GURU99!'.
Stack:
    Error: Failed expectation
        at Object.<anonymous> (C:\Users\RE041943\Desktop\guru\spec.js:10:24)
        at C:\Users\RE041943\AppData\Roaming\npm\node_modules\protractor\node_modules\jasmine
        at new wrappedCtr (C:\Users\RE041943\AppData\Roaming\npm\node_modules\protractor\node
        at controlFlowExecute (C:\Users\RE041943\AppData\Roaming\npm\node_modules\protractor\
        at goog.async.run.processWorkQueue (C:\Users\RE041943\AppData\Roaming\npm\node_module
        at process._tickCallback (node.js:369:9)

1 spec, 1 failure
Finished in 11.021 seconds
[launcher] 0 instance(s) of WebDriver still running
[launcher] chrome #1 failed 1 test(s)
[launcher] overall: 1 failed spec(s)
[launcher] Process exited with error code 1

C:\Users\RE041943\Desktop\guru>
```

We can see the result as failed indicated with 'F' in the screenshot with the reason as **"Expected 'Hello GURU99!' to equal 'Hello change GURU99!'.** Also, it shows how many failures is encountered when executing code.

Can we achieve the same with Selenium web driver?

Sometimes we can identify the web elements of AngularJS applications using XPath or CSS selector from Selenium web driver. But in AngularJS applications, the elements will be generated and changed dynamically. So Protractor is the better practice to work with AngularJS applications.

Generate Reports using Jasmine Reporters

Protractor supports Jasmine reporters to generate test reports. In this section, we will use JunitXMLReporter to generate Test execution reports automatically in XML format.

Follow the below steps to generate reports in XML format.

Installation of Jasmine Reporter

There are two way you can do this, locally or globally

1. Open command prompt execute the following command to install locally

```
npm install --save-dev jasmine-reporters@^2.0.0
```

Above command will install jasmine reports node-modules locally means from the directory where we are running the command in command prompt.

2. Open command prompt execute the following command for global installation

```
npm install -g jasmine-reporters@^2.0.0
```

In this tutorial, we will install the jasmine reporters locally.

Step 1) Execute the command.

```
npm install --save-dev jasmine-reporters@^2.0.0
```

from the command prompt like below.

```
C:\Users\RE041943>cd Desktop
C:\Users\RE041943\Desktop>cd guru
C:\Users\RE041943\Desktop\guru>npm install --save-dev jasmine-reporters@^2.0.0
jasmine-reporters@2.0.0 node_modules\jasmine-reporters
└── mkdirp@0.3.5
C:\Users\RE041943\Desktop\guru>
```

Step 2) Check the installation folders in the directory. " Node_modules" should be available if it is successfully installed like in below snapshot.

result	3/15/2016 6:24 PM	File folder	
node_modules	3/16/2016 9:39 PM	File folder	
E Ranjith kumar .txt	3/16/2016 9:51 PM	Text Document	1 KB

Step 3) Add the following colored code to an existed conf.js file

```
exports.config = {
    seleniumAddress: 'http://localhost:4444/wd/hub',
    capabilities: {
        'browserName': 'firefox'
    },
```

```
      specs: ['spec.js'],
    framework: 'jasmine2' ,
     onPrepare: function() {
         var jasmineReporters =
require('C:/Users/RE041943/Desktop/guru/node_modules/jasmine-
reporters');
         jasmine.getEnv().addReporter(new
jasmineReporters.JUnitXmlReporter(null, true, true)
         );
     }
  };
```

Explanation of code:

In code, we are generating the report "**JUnitXmlReporter**" and giving the Path where to store the report.

Step 4) Open the command prompt and execute command **protractor conf.js.**

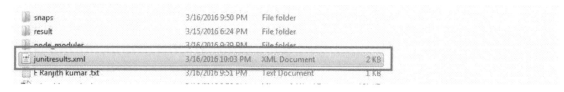

```
C:\Users\RE041943\Desktop\guru>protractor conf.js
Using the selenium server at http://localhost:4444/wd/hub
[launcher] Running 1 instances of WebDriver
Started


Failures:
1) Enter GURU99 Name should add a Name as GURU99
  Message:
    Expected 'Hello GURU99' to equal 'Hello change GURU99'.
  Stack:
    Error: Failed expectation
        at Object.<anonymous> (C:\Users\RE041943\Desktop\guru\spec.js:10:24)
        at C:\Users\RE041943\AppData\Roaming\npm\node_modules\protractor\node_
        at new wrappedCtr (C:\Users\RE041943\AppData\Roaming\npm\node_modules
        at controlFlowExecute (C:\Users\RE041943\AppData\Roaming\npm\node_mod
        at goog.async.run.processWorkQueue (C:\Users\RE041943\AppData\Roaming
        at process._tickCallback (node.js:369:9)

1 spec, 1 failure
Finished in 17.696 seconds
```

Step 5) When you execute the above code, junitresults.xml will be generated in mentioned path.

snaps	3/16/2016 9:50 PM	File folder	
result	3/15/2016 6:24 PM	File folder	
node_modules	3/16/2016 9:39 PM	File folder	
junitresults.xml	3/16/2016 10:03 PM	XML Document	2 KB
F Ranjith kumar .txt	3/16/2016 9:51 PM	Text Document	1 KB

Step 6) Open the XML and verify the result. The failure message is shown in the result file as our Test Case is failed. The Test case is failed

as because of the Expected Result from "spec.js" is not matched with the Actual result from a Web page

Step 7) Use the junitresult.xml file for evidences or result files.

Summary:

Though Selenium can do some of the things what protractor does, the protractor is the industrial standard and best practice to test AngularJS applications. A Protractor can also manage multiple capabilities in it and handle the dynamic changes of web elements using ng-model, ng-click.., etc.. (Which selenium cannot do).

Made in the USA
Middletown, DE
22 February 2019